P9-APS-673

JOEY YAP'S
PURE
FENG SHUI

BRING ABUNDANCE TO YOUR HOME,
HAPPINESS TO YOUR RELATIONSHIPS,
AND SUCCESS TO YOUR CAREER

RYLAND
PETERS
& SMALL
LONDON NEW YORK

Published in 2008 by Ryland Peters & Small
20–21 Jockey's Fields   519 Broadway, 5th Floor
London WC1R 4BW   New York, NY 10012
www.rylandpeters.com

10 9 8 7 6 5 4 3 2 1

Text © Joey Yap 2008
Design and illustrations © Ryland Peters & Small 2008

The author's moral rights have been asserted. All rights reserved. No part of this publication may
be reproduced, stored in a retrieval system, or transmitted in any form or by any means, electronic, mechanical,
photocopying, or otherwise, without the prior permission of the publisher.

A CIP catalog record for this book is available from the Library of Congress and the British Library.

ISBN-13: 978 1 906094 96 6

Printed in China

Editor: Alison Wormleighton
Design: Jerry Goldie
Illustration: Trina Dalziel
Picture Research: Emily Westlake
Cover illustration: Stephen Dew

Picture credits

Red Cover Picture Library: all of the following images © Redcover.com
pp. 5: Grant Govier; 14: Christopher Drake; 18: Ed Reeve; 21: Ken Hayden; 35: Paul Massey; 40: Chris Tubbs;
46: Quickimage/Emilio Rodriguez; 49: Grey Crawford; 130: Winfried Heinze; 135: Michael Freeman; 137: Bieke Claessens;
144: Grant Scott; 148: Verity Welstead; 169: Karyn Millet, Designer: The Warwick Group.

All of the following images © Ryland Peters & Small. Key: ph= photographer.
pp. 42, ph Jan Baldwin/a family home in London, architecture by Nicholas Helm and Yasuyuki Fukuda of Helm Architects
(www.helmarchitects.com), interior design and all material finishes supplied by Maria Speake of Retrouvius Reclamation
& Design (www.retrouvius.com); 54, ph Polly Wreford/home of architect Reinhard Weiss & Bele Weiss in London
(www.3sarchitects.com); 58, ph Chris Everard/Ben Atfield's house in London; 64, ph Polly Wreford/Siobhán McKeating's
home in London (www.brissi.co.uk); 72, ph Polly Wreford/Abigail Ahern's home in London (www.atelierabigailahern.com);
83, ph Polly Wreford/Abigail Ahern's home in London (www.atelierabigailahern.com); 94, ph Polly Wreford/Alex White;
103, ph Melanie Eclaire/Fovant Hut Garden near Salisbury in Wiltshire created by garden designer Christina Oates
together with her husband Nigel (www.secretgardendesigns.co.uk); 105, ph Polly Wreford /Foster House (at
www.beachstudios.co.uk); 106, ph Polly Wreford/Charlotte-Anne Fidler's home in London; 113, ph Polly Wreford/
(www.beachstudios.co.uk); 116, ph Dan Duchars/architect Haifa Hammami's home in London (07730 307612);
121, ph Dan Duchars/architect Haifa Hammami's home in London (07730 307612); 129, ph Polly Wreford/London home
of Michael Bains and Catherine Woram (www.catherineworam.co.uk); 136, ph Andrea Jones; 142, ph Winfried Heinze;
149, ph Debi Treloar/architect Simon Colebrook's home in London (www.dspl.co.uk); 150, ph Debi Treloar/a country house
rebuilt and extended by James Gorst Architects (www.jamesgorstarchitects.co.uk); 154, ph Polly Wreford/Ingrid and
Avinash Persaud's home in London (www.mmarchitects.com); 160, ph Andrew Wood/Eero Aarnio's house in Veikkola,
Finland (www.eero-aarnio.com); 165, ph Jan Baldwin/designer Chester Jones' house in London; 167, ph Polly Wreford/
Foster House (at www.beachstudios.co.uk); 170, ph Ray Main/Robert Callender & Elizabeth Ogilvie's studio in Fife
designed by John C Hope Architects (Edinburgh 0131 315 2215).

CONTENTS

Introduction:
The Truth about Feng Shui

Pure feng shui is based on compass directions, not the placement of objects in the home.

In the beginning...

There were no mandarin ducks. There were no Ba Gua mirrors. There were no eight life aspiration sectors. There was no Universal Love Corner in the southwest. There were no ships carrying gold, resin dragons, or peony paintings.

In the beginning, there were the yin and yang, the eight trigrams, and the five elements.

In the beginning, feng shui was not for the living—it was mainly for the dead. Feng shui was for graves and burial sites, not homes and offices. Feng shui masters served the emperor, the imperial family, imperial officers, and high officials, not the layperson.

And then there was evolution

Gradually, the tenets of feng shui, established in the numerous classical texts dating back to the Tang dynasty (618–907), were extended to living spaces. And at the turn of the century, as China moved away from feudalism, new attitudes prevailed in the field of feng shui.

Once upon a time, feng shui masters clung to the mantra that "the secrets of the heavens are never revealed." Masters zealously guarded their trade secrets, passing on the knowledge only on their deathbed. Even then, they passed it on only to disciples who were sworn to uphold the credo of their master's school of feng shui.

As China entered the twentieth century, feng shui masters began to teach feng shui openly, in schools that anyone with an interest in it and a willingness to learn could attend. With the fall of the Qing dynasty in 1911, feng shui masters had no imperial family and imperial officers to serve. Like the bakers and chefs of the French bourgeoisie, who started up their own bakeries and restaurants after the fall of the French royal family in the French Revolution, they began to ply their trade to the layperson and businessmen. When the People's Republic was founded in 1949, feng shui was discouraged and at times banned in China, so the masters moved to Taiwan and Hong Kong, paving the way for those two countries to become the powerhouses of feng shui practice and study.

Along came the renaissance

In the 1990s, feng shui emerged in the Western world as an exotic, ancient practice, shrouded in the mysticism of the East, and touted as the answer to all one's woes. This mystique was further enhanced by its

Pure feng shui means going with your own style—and not having your home look like a Chinese supermarket.

link with the imperial dynasties of China, and the business tycoons of Hong Kong and Taiwan. Feng shui has the intoxicating allure of being able to create empires, take you from rags to riches, and make all your dreams come true.

Since feng shui, for all intents and purposes, was until that point largely confined to an audience capable of reading Chinese texts, the emergence of English language books on the subject revived interest in feng shui, even among Asians. But along with the revolution came commercialism.

The science of harnessing the qi of the environment for the purpose of achieving one's goals in life somehow became "the art of object placement." Feng shui cures became commonplace, available at the nearest corner store. Making use of feng shui became not much more than a matter of placing the right object in the right corner.

> *"This is a feng shui that doesn't lecture you on the colors you should have in your home"*

At the cusp of revolution

Today, the practice of feng shui has become inextricably associated with lucky objects, symbols, cultural superstition, and, increasingly, aspiration and positive thinking. It has also become tainted by commercialism and a retail component.

Fortunately, I believe that we are at the start of a feng shui revolution. This revolution seeks to go back to basics and looks toward the application of authentic feng shui, utilizing classical theories and applications, as written in the ancient classics of the Tang (618–907), Sung (960–1279), Ming (1368–1644), and Qing (1644–1911) dynasties. It is a revolution that looks to utilize feng shui, without object placement and free of cultural elements and superstition.

In short, this is a feng shui that doesn't lecture you on the colors you should have in your home, the furniture you should buy, the pendants you need to wear, or which corner your mandarin ducks must be placed in. It is a feng shui that doesn't require you to engage in expensive retail therapy, and doesn't depend on how good you are at positive thinking—it's a feng shui that creates real results, quickly. It is pure feng shui.

Why are you reading this book?

Let me be a little bold and suggest that you are probably reading this book for one or more of the reasons below. And if you're not reading it for these reasons, then maybe you should be...

- You want a system of feng shui that works, please!
- You want to understand more about the type of feng shui that you are practicing, so that you can determine what kind of results you get.
- You want to have a broader perspective of feng shui, beyond feng shui as the "art of object placement."
- You want to understand the feng shui mindset, which is the attitude needed to make feng shui work for you, and help you achieve your goals.
- You want to advance in your study of feng shui and want to know how to move forward, without being confused or finding you have contradictory knowledge that you cannot reconcile.

Placing objects such as a wealth buddha in your home won't make you money.

I have written *Pure Feng Shui* with all these goals, and the feng shui revolution, in mind.

The book will take you back to basics on the subject of classical feng shui, as it was practiced from the Tang dynasty all the way through the Sung, Ming, and Qing dynasties, and as it is practiced today in its homelands, Hong Kong and Taiwan. More importantly, the book is about feng shui that is unadulterated by "retail-ism" and commercialism.

At the same time, I am deeply mindful that I must address the needs of a range of readers. Some will be new to feng shui, while others will have been practicing it for some time. Feng shui practitioners come in all forms—professionals, talented amateurs, aficionados, and even intellectuals, who are inclined more toward its theoretical aspect. While this book cannot address all these groups of people individually, I hope that whichever category you fall into, you will find this book both practical and inspiring—and that the logical, rational approach taken here, and the many sections on debunking various feng shui myths, will broaden your understanding of the practice of feng shui.

What other books won't tell you

The information that goes into a book on feng shui is as important as what is left out. Here are some of the inconvenient truths that usually don't make it into most feng shui books.

They won't tell you what feng shui is

Defining feng shui is an extremely difficult task—not because it is a slippery subject that defies definition, but because the add-ons to the subject have made it become something that is all things to all people, and anything and everything. The word "feng shui" has become synonymous with everything New Age, alternative, unorthodox and unconventional.

Yet defining a subject is an integral part of any book. In Chapter 1, I will tackle how to define feng shui and explain to you how you can separate the various types of feng shui, based on their approach, and also on their measurable outcomes and results.

They won't tell you that feng shui is a complicated subject

On the theoretical side, it has elements of metaphysics, existentialism, and philosophy, all melded into one. And when you throw in the practical aspect, which requires skills like problem-solving, intellectualizing problems, understanding business models, and trouble-shooting as well as engaging in life-planning, its complexity emerges.

But while feng shui is a complicated subject, it can be practiced on either a simple level or a sophisticated level. It is a subject of great complexity, but also great simplicity. The key is to play at the level you're at, and within your understanding.

Feng shui is not a religion

Misconceptions about feng shui and how it relates to religion are among the leading causes of skepticism about feng shui. They are a compelling reason why people of faith as well as agnostics and even atheists find it hard to give feng shui a try.

New Age feng shui is largely the reason for these misconceptions. Certain practices that have sprung out of it have led to the perception of feng shui as being on a par with the occult, with its chanting, rituals, prayers, and, most significantly, emphasis on "believing" or having faith in the practice in order for it to work.

The perception that you have to worship an object or put your faith in an object also strikes many people as paganish. Since some of these objects are derived from Buddhist, Taoist, or Tibetan religious and symbolic practice, it is hard for people of other faiths to accept this. Naturally, it's all the more damning as far as the agnostics and atheists are concerned.

The truth is that (although you have to buy into the concept, of course) feng shui is faith-free, and religion-free.

They won't tell you that feng shui is not an ancient art

It isn't—unless you consider a thousand years old to be ancient. Indeed, the flying stars system, which has been the subject of many feng shui books, is only about 150 years old.

They won't tell you that feng shui is not about products, Chinese or otherwise

Feng shui doesn't require you to change your religion, become a Sinophile, adopt Eastern habits and ideas, or turn your home into a miniature version of the Forbidden City, replete with unicorns, lion heads, and dragon motifs on every wall.

They won't tell you about needing to know what you want in life

Feng shui is a goal-oriented practice. Believe it or not, you need to know what you want before you can make good use of feng shui. Most books skim over this highly practical aspect of using it.

In this book I will ask you to clearly identify the goal or objective that you want to achieve, in accordance with a list of possible issues associated with the four main life aspiration areas (Wealth, Career, Relationships, and Health). Then I will show you how to use feng shui to achieve that goal.

They won't talk about the astrology factor

The cosmic trinity (see the illustration, overleaf) is not included in many feng shui books. The concept of this is that success is derived from a combination of three factors: man luck (your own actions, beliefs, and behavior), heaven luck (your astrological chart, or destiny code), and earth luck (your feng shui).

Feng shui constitutes only 33 percent of the equation for success in life—the earth luck factor. Your capacity for success, in whatever area you want, is also dictated to the extent of 33 percent by what is known as your destiny code—this is the heaven luck factor. And your own efforts (perseverance, patience, persistence, hard work, determination, for example)—the man luck factor—account for 33 percent of the outcome as well.

"Feng shui doesn't require you to change your religion"

So while feng shui is important, it is not the be-all and end-all. It is not an overriding factor that can trump everything else. Nor is it a miracle cure, no matter how "potent" the system is. Your personal astrology or destiny also comes into play.

They won't explain anything

Many feng shui books do not explain the basis of their methods or techniques. These are often called trade secrets or ancient secrets passed down only to in-house apprentices or disciples.

In this book, where appropriate, I explain the theoretical underpinnings of a method or an application. Sometimes, though, to keep things simple I just show you how to use the application, as this book ultimately is about helping you achieve your goals through feng shui. But that doesn't mean that you shouldn't be interested in how feng shui works to help you achieve these goals.

In the following chapters, I make it clear which system my techniques or methods are drawn from—either flying stars or San He (Three Harmony) feng shui—and I give you background information on the different systems.

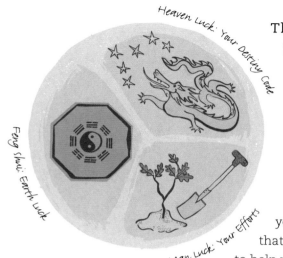

Heaven Luck: Your Destiny Code

Feng Shui: Earth Luck

Man Luck: Your Efforts

The "cosmic trinity" of heaven luck, earth luck, and man luck. Each sector influences 33 percent of your life.

What this book will do for you

- Give you simple, easy-to-use techniques to help you solve specific problems.
- Walk you through the process of activating certain types of qi in your home to help you achieve your goals.
- Explain the outcomes you can expect and any incidental effects.
- Give you a time frame in which to expect an outcome.
- Show you the techniques used by professionals to insure that you demarcate your property correctly and appropriately.

My goal is to encourage you to think about feng shui in a different way—in a pure feng shui way. In doing so, I will sometimes be taking a provocative stance. I might even go so far as to state that certain feng shui practices are downright wrong, and tell you why they are wrong (look out for the Myth or Truth? features throughout the book).

However, the ultimate goal of this book is to show you how feng shui, when it is used correctly, can produce real, tangible results. So, it is not all theory, debunking, and challenging conventions. The techniques that I will share with you are easy to use, effective, and, crucially, personalized to you and you alone. You won't be getting a generic feng shui "cure-all" but a personalized solution, tailored specifically to your problem or aspiration.

How does classical feng shui work?

Classical feng shui operates on the premise that if there is good qi flow throughout the area, and the property—be it one with a lot of land or a high-rise property—is receiving benevolent, positive qi, then the occupants of the property feel better, sleep better, and live better, and so are better able to achieve their goals in life.

First, you need good qi in the environment. Next, your property needs to receive this qi. Finally, the layout of the home needs to be conducive, encouraging qi to permeate all the rooms and to meander and circulate around the property.

The philosophy of feng shui is really simple. Find the good qi. Tap the good qi. Circulate the good qi.

Making feng shui work for you is a matter of making sure that you have the qi, that you are using the right variety of feng shui (the kind that is about tapping into the qi of the environment, not the kind that is about figurines, objects, trinkets, crystals, and symbolism), and, most importantly, that you always keep it simple.

"The philosophy of feng shui is really simple. Find the good qi. Tap the good qi. Circulate the good qi"

In this book, I will introduce you to a lot of techniques and practical applications, but they are all based on either the San He (Three Harmony) system or the flying stars system. This keeps things simple and straightforward and helps you get results in a timely, effective fashion. Yes, it means you won't get a technique from every system out there, but it will insure you get the outcomes you want.

When you say classical, don't you mean "old-fashioned"?

The term "classical feng shui" is my label for feng shui that comes from the original texts and scripts. Some people think classical means out of date. Well, I don't think classical music is out of date. In fact, it has become associated with something that lasts the test of time and has a timeless quality to it. It remains relevant and rings true, through the ages—as do the subjects called the Classics still taught at some universities. It is also why the works of Aristotle, Shakespeare, and Machiavelli continue to be relevant in this day and age. That which is classical is not always out of date, irrelevant, or insignificant—far from it.

Some books say that classical feng shui is not relevant to modern living because it does not take into account apartments or high-rise buildings. But although classical feng shui refers to the use of classical theories as the foundation for the practice of feng shui, the application has been adapted to modern situations. Accordingly, whether it's a house or an apartment, a skyscraper or a mall, a theme park or a resort, classical feng shui can be applied with ease.

> "Classical feng shui involves no rituals, chants, prayers, or objects. It doesn't require you to believe in it in order for it to work"

Why should I use classical feng shui?

Would you like people to know you're using feng shui? What bigger giveaway is there than having a house full of oriental knickknacks occupying every nook and cranny? Classical feng shui is nuanced and effective, but more importantly, it is practical.

- It involves minimal cost and investment, and the techniques and methods discussed here will involve few, if any, renovations or modifications to your home.
- You will not be required to buy anything beyond perhaps a compass, and an aquarium or modest water feature if you want to use Water to activate certain sectors.
- You don't have to compromise your religious beliefs—classical feng shui involves no rituals, chants, prayers, or objects. It doesn't require you to believe in it in order for it to work.

- You will make use of what is already in your home—the rooms, the doors, and the qi already present.
- You don't have to keep changing or updating your good luck objects or elemental cures.
- The techniques and methods outlined in this book are utilized by practitioners but, most importantly, have been written to insure safety. They will not result in negative or undesirable outcomes, even if incorrectly implemented. In short, you won't get more trouble for your trouble!
- You get timely, positive outcomes, tailored to your specific problem and personalized to you, and you alone.
- It's easy if you know how!

Is the sky the limit?

Let me keep it real for you right from the start. Since this book is all about giving you a true picture of feng shui, here it is.

As this is a basic book, it is confined to internal feng shui, which is done inside a property. I do not delve into the issue of your environment and the quality of qi in the area that you live in. Yet this is perhaps the most important factor that affects the extent to which feng shui can work for you.

I maintain, however, that one should never be discouraged by one's circumstances or allow what cannot be altered to prevent change. Do what you can and endeavor to make the best of your circumstances. Remember the cosmic trinity? By activating the correct sectors of your home, and with a little help from feng shui, you can work toward being in a position where you live in an area with positive qi.

Do not discount the 33 percent contribution of feng shui, and never let what you can't do prevent you from doing something. Make the effort, strive to be all that you can be, and let classical feng shui help you get to that level.

Chapter 1
Feng Shui Fundamentals

Before you can begin to tap into the energies in your home, you need to get to know some of the important principles of feng shui. Even if you are already familiar with feng shui, do read this chapter. The commercialization of feng shui in recent years has resulted in many key concepts and principles being oversimplified or exaggerated. When you truly understand the basics, and become confident in your understanding, you will be able to make changes that show real results.

Feng shui: beyond mere wind and water

To set you on the right path toward understanding feng shui and being able to achieve good results, we begin by answering a very simple but important question: what is feng shui?

Feng shui, when dissected, means "wind" (feng) and "water" (shui). This is an explanation that can be found in most Western books on the subject. Unfortunately, it is a perfunctory answer at best and doesn't really answer the question. It doesn't explain the connection to wind and water either.

Feng shui wasn't always called this. Nor was it originally about homes, living space, and tapping into the energies of the universe for the benefit of the living—it was actually about the study of graves and burial grounds.

During the Tang dynasty (618–907), a field of study emerged that was known as Kan Yu, which translates as "the study of the heavens and earth." A metaphysical discipline, Kan Yu essentially was the practice of identifying good burial spots, utilizing the basic principles of yin and yang. It was only during the Sung, Ming, and Qing dynasties that the theories and principles of Kan Yu were applied beyond graves and burial spots, to living areas and homes. So the ancient art of feng shui is really only as "ancient" as a thousand years old.

The term "feng shui" itself is only about a hundred years old, having come into use to refer to the study of Kan Yu. No one really knows why "Kan Yu" stopped being used and "feng shui" became prevalent. One of the origins of the phrase "feng shui" is thought to be the famous Chinese classical text on graves called the *Burial Book*, by the sage Kuo Pu. The *Burial Book* says: "Qi is dispersed by wind, and collects at the boundaries of water."

The Ba Gua, or eight-trigrams model used by feng shui practitioners (see also page 27).

However, this is probably not where the name "feng shui" comes from. A likely explanation is that as Kan Yu involved the observation of the winds and also the water mouth, it was abbreviated to "wind" and "water," thus feng shui. Another possible explanation is that the term comes from a rude retort whenever a person is thought to be looking around but observing nothing. In such an instance, the person is said to be "looking at wind and water."

Thus the name feng shui does not really define it in a meaningful way, especially since the origins of the term itself are unclear. So just what is feng shui?

Today, it can be virtually anything. It is lumped together with the metaphysical, the alternative, the transformational, and the just plain kooky. It is space clearing, it is crystal therapy, it is holistic energies. The term "feng shui" seems to add an instant magical credibility to any idea. As a result, there are so many different versions of feng shui being practiced today that there simply is no single answer to the question of what it is.

Classifying the types of feng shui

To distinguish between the various types of feng shui, we need to have some means to differentiate them or perhaps group them. One way that I find useful is to see whether they fall into the categories of classical feng shui or New Age feng shui.

Feng shui means "wind" and "water."

Classical feng shui is the term I use to refer to feng shui that utilizes the theories and principles found in many of the ancient texts on Kan Yu written from the time of the Tang dynasty. Based on the use of specific formulas to compute the qi map of a property, it employs the observation of landforms (such as mountains and rivers) to determine the location of qi spots, which are essentially planetary energy or meridian points. It taps into the energies of the environment through the use of location (where a room or house is placed) or direction (which way the main door, desk, bed, and stove in a house are facing).

New Age feng shui is the term I use to categorize varieties of feng shui that are chiefly identifiable by their reliance on lucky objects, auspicious items, good luck symbols, cultural myths, crystals, space clearing, color therapy, and aspirational and transformational concepts. New Age feng shui is heavily oriented around the use of ornaments and objects and is often described as "the art of object placement." Most of the practices and techniques in New Age feng shui are feng shui science fiction—they may have a link to classical feng shui (such as elemental

Classical feng shui allows you to practice feng shui in a way that suits your personal style, without changing your color scheme.

cures) but most are largely speculative and involve extrapolation without any theoretical basis.

Many of the principles, methods, and techniques in New Age feng shui are aspirational and transformational derivatives of the ancient Chinese manual the *Yi Jing* (known in the West as the *I Ching*, or Book of Changes) and the Ba Gua (see page 27). A large number of New Age feng shui "cures" are drawn from symbolism and cultural superstition rather than feng shui conventions. For example, mandarin ducks are often cited as a feng shui cure for a poor love life. Mandarin ducks represent romance for the Chinese because these ducks symbolize matrimonial harmony. But they are not feng shui in any sense of the word, since the mandarin duck figurines do not emit any qi or actually alter the qi in your room or property.

In other words, New Age feng shui is much less about authentic feng shui techniques and methods, as practiced since the Tang dynasty, and much more about pop psychology, superstition, and old wives' tales. Sometimes, it's nothing more than an attempt to encourage positive thinking.

All of the fundamental principles and the techniques that you will read about in this book are rooted in classical feng shui.

The great classical feng shui debate

Within classical feng shui, there are two major schools of thought or movements—the San He school or movement and the San Yuan school or movement. The San Yuan ("Three Cycles") system is a mathematical model of the Ba Gua that is used to calculate the quality of qi through time. San Yuan involves updating one's feng shui to keep up with the qi cycle and adopting a dynamic approach to stay in tandem with the changing qi. By contrast, San He ("Three Harmony") focuses on the environment—the mountains, the rivers, and the landforms—and aims to understand how nature shapes, creates, and fosters qi, in order to find an optimal or strategic location in which to benefit from the qi in the environment. San He recognizes that qi is dynamic and changes through time, but looks to insulate and outlast any unfavorable periods in the qi cycle through superior landform and house structure.

Up until about a hundred years ago, most feng shui masters practiced either San He or San Yuan feng shui exclusively. Today, most masters utilize the two systems in tandem. Both San Yuan and San He involve methods and techniques to tap into the natural energies, or qi, in your environment and harness those energies to support your goals. That is what classical feng shui is all about. Rather than quibbling over which system to use, one should focus on using what is most suitable for the situation at hand. Indeed, the techniques

The types of classical feng shui

- Flying stars (Fei Xing)
- Eight Mansions (Ba Zhai)
- Three Harmony (San He)
- Three Cycles (San Yuan)
- 64 Hexagrams (Xuan Kong Da Gua)

Classical feng shui is also always practiced in tandem with Chinese astrology, such as Four Pillars of Destiny (BaZi) or Purple Star (Zi Wei) astrology, and complemented by disciplines like physiognomy, or face reading, and date selection.

covered in this book are a mixture of the San He and San Yuan approaches. The key is to utilize one system or the other consistently, and not try to make feng shui chop suey.

Classical feng shui essentials

Classical feng shui is a subject of incredible depth, sophistication, and complexity. But at the same time it can be simple and minimalist. It has a soaring, highly intellectual theoretical basis, yet is also very practical in its application.

"The techniques covered in this book are a mixture of the San He and San Yuan approaches. The key is to utilize one system or the other consistently, and not try to make feng shui chop suey"

As with any subject, you need to know the big picture but also have a grasp of the details. In classical feng shui, the big picture is the metaphysical foundation, what I call the core theories, while the details relate to the practical understanding needed to apply the theories, what I call the core basics.

Core theories involve an understanding of qi and landforms, and the concepts of yin and yang, the Ba Gua, and the five elements, or the trinity of classical feng shui. Core basics revolve around the practical details and skills, such as an appreciation of the difference between direction and location, understanding how qi moves and flows, and applying these concepts to your home.

Always be aware of the features, or external forms, outside your property.

Core theories

The heart of classical feng shui is simply about tapping into qi to benefit oneself. But what is this qi thing?

Chichi qi

You will have already seen in this book many references to energies of the environment, or qi. But qi (sometimes written as chi) is a word that has lost its meaning. With the advent of New Age feng shui, it seems anything and everything is capable of emitting qi. We certainly live in an energy-laden world, where everything from a potted plant to a wooden shelf is emitting qi, so that it is coming at us from every direction.

In classical feng shui, qi refers to the natural energies found in the environment, which arise from the fusion of yin (Mountain) and yang (Water).

At the basic level, all qi can be classified as either sheng qi (or growth qi) and sha qi (or killing qi). Simplistically, in classical feng shui we like sheng qi, and we don't like sha qi. The goal of classical feng shui is simply to tap or harness the sheng qi and to avoid the sha qi. Contrary to popular misconception, it is not necessary to neutralize or cure sha qi. If one can avoid it entirely in the first place and thus not have a problem, then there's no need to cure, neutralize, or fix it.

"Contrary to popular misconception, it is not necessary to neutralize or cure sha qi. If one can avoid it entirely in the first place and not have a problem, then there's no need to cure, neutralize, or fix it"

Real qi or no qi

From a strictly purist standpoint, only natural land formations can emit and produce qi. Artificial and man-made structures cannot emit or produce it.

As we now live in a world where there are more man-made structures than there are natural land formations, classical feng shui has evolved slightly to take into account the presence of man-made objects. However, this is only insofar as such objects may block or redirect sheng qi, transform sheng qi into sha qi, or simply emit sha qi.

Man-made objects are also only taken into consideration when they are large. How do we define large? The little pile of rocks in your garden would not be considered a sufficiently large man-made object to influence the qi of your property. But a structure like, say, the Statue of Liberty or a skyscraper would be taken into consideration.

Whenever we ask the question of whether or not there is qi in a particular environment or location, we always look first at real mountains (including hills and knolls) and real water (such as rivers, ponds, and creeks). Man-made structures have an influence, but these are secondary to natural formations.

Qi flow and movement

Like water, qi flows from high to low, meanders slowly, or flows in a focused, forceful manner. Qi can pool in an area but it can also dissipate. It can be collected, and it can be distributed, just like water. It can be squeezed and it can also be expanded.

Front door

Hall qi flow

Qi, or energy, flows from high to low, from upper floors to lower floors. In halls or corridors, qi ideally meanders through the space.

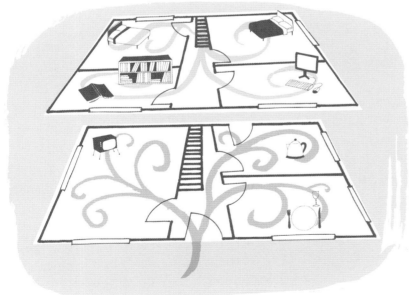

Upper Floor

Lower Floor

In classical feng shui, qi flow must always be "sentimental." This means that the qi moves in a meandering, slow manner and has the opportunity to circulate around the property. When qi flow is not "sentimental," it is "merciless" and thus becomes sha qi.

- Qi pools and collects in open spaces. Open spaces in your home, like the area in front of your main door or your living area, should be bright and uncluttered, to encourage the pooling and collection of qi.
- In narrow spaces, qi is squeezed and focused so that it moves rapidly. Thus, narrow spaces like halls should ideally be short. If they are long, they should also be broad to encourage the qi to meander and move slowly.
- Qi flows downward and never upward. Thus, qi on an upper story of a building is always more passive or calm than qi on the ground floor. This is why it is always better to locate bedrooms and studies upstairs, and to locate active areas like the living room or television room on the ground floor, where the qi is more active.
- Airless rooms result in stagnant qi, so it is good to open the windows occasionally and allow qi to circulate.

Landforms: the makers of qi

"External landforms are the source of qi in an environment"

Qi itself is inexorably linked to landforms, often abbreviated just to forms. The Chinese for landforms is Luan Tou, which translates as "the face of the mountain." Landforms can be used to reference external landforms (real mountains, hills, or contours in the land and real water) or internal landforms, which relate to sharp corners, beams, or sloping features within the interior of a property.

At the beginner stage, it is important to appreciate that external landforms are the source of qi in an environment. Thus, without external landforms in an area, there is either stagnant qi or no qi. As a rule of thumb, it is best to avoid living in an area that is devoid of either natural water (such as a lake, pond, stream, or even modern irrigation) or natural contours (such as hills and mountains).

There are very few places in the world that are completely flat—even gentle contours in the land mean it is not flat. So do not panic if you cannot physically see a mountain or hill. When you drive around your neighborhood and the roads slope downward or upward, you have contours in the land. To keep things simple, we'll leave external land-forms out of the equation for now. But be aware that they have an important role in the bigger picture.

In this book, the focus is on using the qi map of the property to locate the sheng qi and sha qi. This keeps things easy, and is simple to implement. Where appropriate, I sometimes suggest that you check for internal forms that may cause sha qi, as it would have a neutralizing effect on the sheng qi. But for simplicity's sake, we'll focus on ascertaining the location of sheng qi and tapping into that sheng qi

The trinity of classical feng shui

Dig deep into any classical feng shui system and you'll find yourself coming back to the three concepts that form the backbone of not just classical feng shui, but also Chinese metaphysics. I call these the trinity of classical feng shui. They are yin and yang, the Ba Gua, and the five elements.

Yin and yang = perfection

In feng shui, the phrase yin and yang is usually used in an all-encompassing manner. Graves are called yin houses, and homes are called yang houses. In landforms, water is the yang force, and mountains are the yin force. A long, dark corridor would be described as being yin, while a broad, bright corridor can be said to be yang. Being passive or introspective is regarded as yin, and being proactive and extrovert is seen as yang. Thought is yin, while action is yang.

The symbol for yin-yang.

At the most basic level, yin and yang refer to two types of energies: unmoving/moving and passive/active. Chinese sages used two brush-strokes to translate these into a visual form: a broken line (yin) and a straight, strong line (yang).

Yin represents the passive, the dark, the feminine, the soft, negative polarity, the internal, and the unseen, among other things. Yang represents the active, the bright, the masculine, the hard, positive polarity, the external, and the seen, among other things.

Chinese sages then added to this the concept of duality. Within all yang there is yin. Within all yin there is yang. Many of the common opposites in life are a manifestation of the duality of yin and yang. Think of night and day, inside and outside, high and low, forward and backward, love and hate, positive and negative, real and false, the conscious and the subconscious.

Yin and yang is essentially an expression of the ideal, or perfection. It is a pictorial representation of the universe in perfect balance, where nothing exists in absolute form. Achieving balance is a matter of finding the tipping point between the two required oppositional forces.

Now let's relate this back to classical feng shui. The goal is to achieve equilibrium or balance between energies. It is to seek the tipping point where the energies in a property are in harmony, perfectly balanced against each other. We don't want to have yin without the yang, or yang without the yin, but yin and yang together.

So how do we apply the concept of yin and yang to the feng shui of a living space? Each area will either be yin or yang. Bedrooms, for example, are yin as that's where we sleep, which is a passive activity. Living rooms are usually yang as that is where most activity takes place. At a simplistic level, feng shui is about determining which rooms have yin energies and which have yang energies, then matching the room to the right energies. Tap into the yin energies for the yin activities or areas, and the yang energies for the yang activities or areas.

On a broader scale, yin and yang relates to mountains (yin) and water (yang). When these two features are found together in the environment, then it can be said that yin and yang are in harmony. At an advanced level of classical feng shui, where we evaluate landforms, an environment devoid of either mountains or water is not considered balanced and so does not have good qi.

"The Ba Gua is an incredibly sophisticated mathematical model of the universe"

The Ba Gua (the eight trigrams)

Most people know of the Ba Gua in the form of the Ba Gua mirror. That, however, is nothing more than an octagonal mirror with Ba Gua lines drawn on it. A Ba Gua mirror has absolutely no connection to the original Ba Gua or feng shui.

The Ba Gua is an incredibly sophisticated mathematical model of the universe, and it is the heart and soul of Chinese metaphysics and classical feng shui. The Ba Gua combines into a single pictorial representation of directions, elements, yin and yang, numerology, and the trigrams. All formulas, theories, and principles of classical feng shui originate in or relate to the Ba Gua and its two incarnations, which are known as the Early Heaven Ba Gua and the Later Heaven Ba Gua.

The classical feng shui subsystem known as Xuan Kong flying stars, for example, is heavily rooted in the Ba Gua. Information within the Ba Gua is the key to determining not just the problem the occupant of a property has, but also how to resolve the problem. The Ba Gua explains the meaning of the stars, and how the qi within the eight sectors interconnects.

For beginners or those new to classical feng shui, it is not essential to have an in-depth knowledge of the Ba Gua. The purpose of introducing you to it is to insure you are aware of the source of the principles, formulas, and applications of classical feng shui—and so that if you seek to advance your knowledge of classical feng shui, the existence of the Ba Gua does not come as a rude shock!

The Ba Gua has eight trigrams, each with an associated compass direction. This is the Later Heaven Ba Gua.

The five elements

Throughout Chinese metaphysics, you will find references to the five elements: Water, Metal, Fire, Earth, and Wood. The Chinese five elements are different from the five elements of Greek metaphysics, which are Fire, Earth, Air, Water, and Ether.

In Chinese metaphysics, the five elements are five types of qi but also five phases of qi, and are integral to the practice and application of disciplines such as feng shui, face reading, and astrology. It is important not only to know what the five elements are, but also to understand the five element theory, which consists of three models, or cycles, of energy transformation and change: the productive cycle, the controlling cycle, and the weakening cycle. At the beginner's level, a basic understanding of how the five elements interact is all that is needed.

The element cycles. The inner circle represents the productive element cycle, the outer circle represents the weakening cycle, and the central arrows show the controlling cycle.

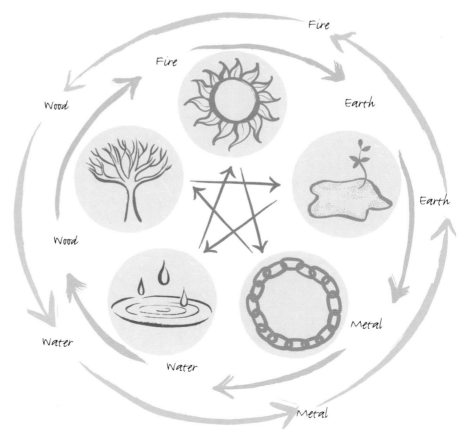

The productive cycle

The productive cycle, which is sometimes known as the forward cycle, is a positive transformation of the energies. In it the five elements interact harmoniously with each other and grow and expand the energies within.

In this cycle, Wood creates Fire and Fire in turn burns substance into ash, producing Earth. From the Earth comes Metal in the form of minerals. Metal, through condensation, attracts Water, which in turn nourishes and grows Wood.

The controlling cycle

The controlling cycle involves the use of the aggressive and oppositional force of one element to control another element.

In this cycle, Water extinguishes or "controls" Fire. Fire in turn melts or controls Metal. Metal cuts Wood, thereby controlling it. Wood in the form of the roots of plants can break the Earth, and thus controls Earth. Earth, meanwhile, is what borders and holds in Water, thus Water is controlled by Earth.

The weakening cycle

The weakening cycle involves an element draining the energies of the element that produces it. This transformation is not a forceful or aggressive process but, rather, a natural use of the manner in which the energies transform between phases.

In this cycle, Wood is nourished by Water; so, Wood weakens Water. Water weakens Metal because Metal produces Water. Earth must be broken up and mined to produce minerals (Metal), thus in the process Metal weakens Earth. Although Fire produces Earth, too much Earth will put out the Fire. Finally, Wood is burned to produce Fire thus Fire weakens Wood.

It is important not to place any bias or prejudice on the three cycles. In classical feng shui, everything has a purpose and every theory has an application. A weakening cycle has its uses, and there are times when we want to use a controlling cycle. Remember yin and yang—freedom and control are both required, it is a matter of finding a tipping point.

"The weakening cycle involves an element draining the energies of the element that produces it"

Core basics

When discussing core theories, I mentioned classical feng shui's philosophical and metaphysical undertones. This aspect of classical feng shui is infinite in its depth and breadth and is best reserved for teahouse conversations.

What really matter are the practical aspects of classical feng shui—the techniques and the application. For these you need what I call core basics: essential basic information and techniques, such as taking a direction and determining the direction and location of various rooms in your living space.

As I will mainly be using methods derived from Xuan Kong flying stars, the core basics here are oriented toward the essentials you will need for applying flying stars feng shui. The core basics of classical feng shui are quite extensive, especially if you are looking to utilize other systems, such as Eight Mansions or San He. But to keep things simple, we will use just the flying stars system. This is not any less effective and, in fact, is more suited to modern living because it is applicable to a wide range of properties, including apartments.

Direction and location

As classical feng shui's primary reference is direction and location, it is important to understand the difference between these two very crucial aspects. Direction in classical feng shui refers to the direction in which you face. Location in classical feng shui is where you are located at that time.

The best way to understand the difference is to take an example. If you were to stand in the center of a square, you could turn to *face* any of the 360 degrees on a compass. However, you would be *located* in the center. Similarly, our imaginary house could have a main door that faced south, but the door itself could be located in, say, the southeast sector.

In classical feng shui terminology, we use the word "sector" or "palace" to denote a location, and we use the word "facing" to denote the direction. So if I were to describe the main door of the property in our

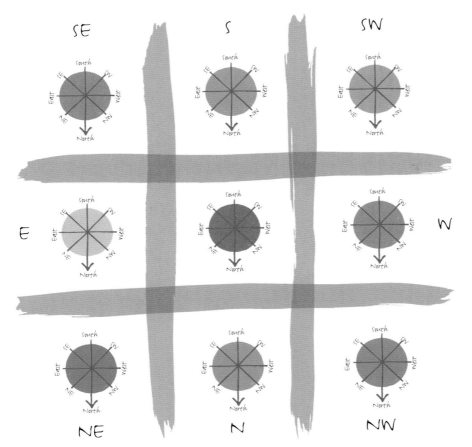

The difference between location and direction: location relates to the compass sector, or palace, of a property, whereas direction is the orientation within that space.

example in classical feng shui terms, I would say that the main door is facing south, but is in the southeast sector. This is applicable to any room and feature in the living space. For example, the study might be located in the north sector, but the door to enter the study could be facing east, and the desk in the southwest subsector, facing west.

What is the significance of direction vs. location?

In classical feng shui, direction and location are the primary methods used to tap into and harness the positive energies in the environment. Formulas are primarily for the purposes of ascertaining the energy map, or qi map, of the property.

Once we have determined what kinds of energies reside in which parts of the property, we can tap into these energies simply by locating a person in that room. The direction is then used for refinement or fine-tuning, to add a higher level of personalization to the process.

In classical feng shui, direction is never prioritized over location. This is because it is possible to face any direction in a given location. Ideally, you would be in a good location, with positive qi, and then face in one of your personal favorable directions. (You have four favorable and four unfavorable directions, based on your Gua number, which in turn is derived from your year of birth. The Gua numbers are shown on page 174. The table on page 176 shows the four favorable directions—sheng qi, tian yi, yan nian, and fu wei—and the four unfavorable directions—huo hai, wu gui, liu sha, and jue ming—for each Gua number. The Guas fall into two groups, east and west.)

If you have a choice between either facing in a personal favorable direction but in a location with negative qi, or being in a good location with positive qi but facing in a personal unfavorable direction, being in the good location is always better than having the good direction.

As you make your way through this book, remember that the old real estate mantra "location, location, location" is an important key to successfully making use of classical feng shui. At all times, you want to be in a good location in your living space first and foremost. Your Personal Favorable Direction should always come second.

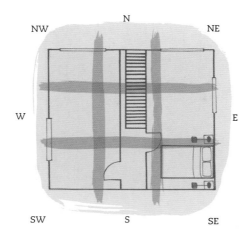

On the left, the bed is located in the southeast sector, placed so the sleeper's head points east. On the floor plan on the right, the bed is still located in the south sector, but this time the bed is orientated south.

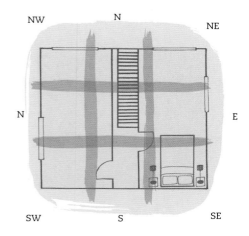

The 24 Mountains

In classical feng shui, the eight directions—north, south, east, west, northeast, northwest, southeast, and southwest—are further subdivided. Thus, within each of the eight main directions, there are three subdirections, resulting in 24 directions, which are known in classical feng shui terminology as the 24 Mountains.

Each of the 24 Mountains spans 15 degrees, and each Mountain corresponds to a trigram or one of the ten Heavenly Stems or twelve Earthly Branches (see page 122). In advanced classical feng shui, we identify the directions by these names. For beginners, it's easier to use numbers to identify the subdirections: northwest 1, northwest 2, northwest 3, south 1, south 2, south 3, and so on.

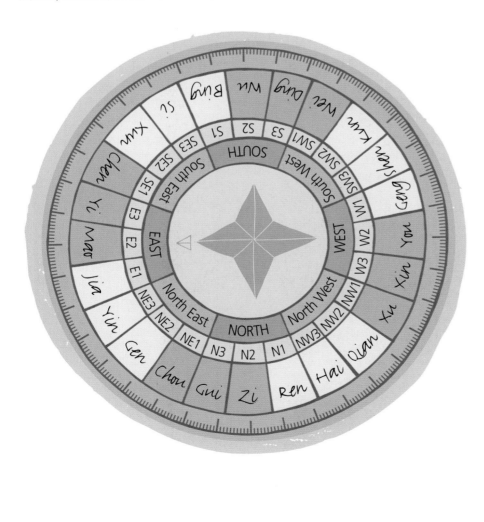

The 24 directions, or Mountains, of the feng shui compass.

The flying stars chart

For many people, the idea of having to plot the flying stars chart of their own property is intimidating. This is especially so for people who are not comfortable with numbers or mathematical computations, even though the process is really not all that mathematical or numerical (there are only nine stars!).

To help make things as simple as possible, I have omitted the need for you to learn how to plot the flying stars chart of your property in order to make use of the techniques and applications discussed in subsequent chapters. Instead, the forty-eight flying stars charts, for all eight directions, in three periods (in other words, sixty years), have been reproduced for your easy reference on pages 76–81.

What you will learn in this section are the basics of reading a flying stars chart. All you will need to be able to do in order to utilize the techniques in this book is:

- Identify the Sitting Stars, Facing Stars, and/or Base Stars in a given chart.
- Remember how to activate the stars.

What is a flying stars chart?

A flying stars chart is essentially a qi map—a map of the energies in a property—according to each sector (north, south, east, west, northeast, northwest, southeast, southwest). The word "star" is really just a way of saying "energy" or "a body of qi."

More than one type of qi can reside in any given sector of a home. Each variant of qi has specific attributes, such as polarity (yin or yang), an area of influence (people matters vs. wealth matters), and an element (Wood, Water, Fire, Metal, or Earth). In classical feng shui we assign numerical values to stars, to make it easier to condense all the relevant information. So, for example, the #4 Star is of the Wood element and relates to learning and people matters. The location of the star, as a Sitting Star, Facing Star, or Base Star, tells us the sphere of influence of the star and the manner in which the star can be utilized or activated. And just as energies can mix together, so the stars can also combine, in what is known as a flying stars combination.

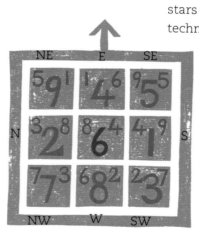

A flying stars chart for a period 6 property, facing E1.

By obtaining the flying stars chart of a property, we are essentially able to determine the areas or rooms in a property with positive qi, and those with negative qi.

Types of flying stars charts

There is a flying stars chart for every day of the month, every month of the year, and every year in a single period, which consists of twenty years. There is also the individual chart of the property, known as the natal flying stars chart. To the untrained person, it is difficult to

However your rooms appear, it is important to look at the flying stars chart for your home to see if their qi will actively enhance your health, prosperity, and romantic happiness.

distinguish between the daily, monthly, annual, and natal charts. So it's important when you get to the practical application chapters in Part Two that you clearly label the charts you are using.

The daily and monthly flying stars charts feature only two stars in each box of the grid. The daily chart changes from day to day, and the monthly chart from month to month. The annual flying stars chart, also known as the yearly flying stars chart, consists only of Base Stars, with one per grid box. This chart remains the same all year, changing only from year to year. Examples of annual charts are shown below.

In Part Two I will show you how to make use of the natal flying stars chart of your property and also the annual flying stars chart. These will enable you to plan the feng shui for your property on both a long-term and a short-term basis and use applications for immediate results, as well as for more gradual, long-term outcomes.

Annual flying stars charts relate just to a calendar year. The chart on the left relates to the years 2001, 2010, and 2019; the chart on the right is for the years 2009 and 2018.

Stars in their palaces

Within each flying stars chart, there are nine boxes. In feng shui parlance, these are known as palaces. There is one palace for each of the eight directions and one for the area in the center, known as the central palace. So what looks like a grid with numbers in it is the chart with the stars in these palaces.

The Base Star is important at advanced levels of classical feng shui, but in this book you will primarily be making use of the Facing Star and the Sitting Star. It is therefore imperative to understand a little bit more about them.

Getting to know the Facing Star

The Facing Star is represented by the number in the top right corner of each palace in a natal flying stars chart (which has three stars in each palace). Facing Stars govern wealth matters—essentially, they are concerned with your finances, and also with your career and with work-related matters.

The Facing Star is sometimes called the Water Star because it is activated by yang action. Yang actions are activities that involve movement. Examples include opening and closing the main door, watching television, and working. Features that have yang qualities include aquariums and small fountains.

In classical feng shui the best way to activate the Facing Star is simply to utilize more the area where it is located. Thus, we like to situate family rooms, television rooms, living rooms, and, where possible, the main door where the Facing Star with positive qi is located.

Getting to know the Sitting Star

The Sitting Star is represented by the number in the top left corner of each palace in a natal flying stars chart. Sitting Stars govern what we call "people matters"—such as relationships, health, and family issues.

The Sitting Star is sometimes called the Mountain Star because it is activated by yin features (like hills and mountains) or yin actions. Yin actions are activities that involve stillness and quiet. Examples of yin actions include sleeping and meditation. Features that have yin qualities include tall cabinets, sculptures, and miniature rock mountains.

In classical feng shui, the best way to activate the Sitting Star is to utilize the area for activities that involve rest, rejuvenation, or thinking. Thus, we like to situate bedrooms, studies, reading rooms, or meditation rooms where the Sitting Star with positive qi is located.

Knowing your animal sign—astrology and feng shui

The final core basic that you will need to know involves the astrological aspect. There is a close relationship between Chinese astrology and classical feng shui methods and techniques. The use of Chinese astrology, such as BaZi or Purple Star astrology, imparts a higher level of personalization to the methods and techniques. In advanced classical feng shui, Chinese astrology is used for diagnostic purposes, and feng shui for prescriptive purposes. A classical feng shui practitioner will ascertain the nature of the person's problems using their astrology chart, and then utilize an appropriate feng shui application to assist them in either resolving the problem or achieving their goal.

Facing Star

Sitting Star

In each palace of a natal flying stars chart there is a principal number which has two small numbers, representing the Sitting Star and Facing Stars.

By cross-referencing your astrological sign (sometimes called your animal sign), you are insuring that the classical feng shui technique you are applying is specific to you alone and is not a generic one-size-fits-all technique or application. This is especially important if you live in a property with several other people, such as friends or family. You want to make sure that the feng shui is targeted toward helping *you* achieve *your* goals.

How to find your astrology sign

There are twelve signs in Chinese astrology: the Rat, Ox, Tiger, Rabbit, Dragon, Snake, Horse, Goat, Monkey, Rooster, Dog, and Pig. Contrary to popular misconception, there is no sign that is "better" or "worse" than another. Your astrology sign is just that, your astrology sign, also known as your animal sign.

Most of the time, establishing your astrology sign is a piece of cake. You simply take your year of birth and refer to the table on page 174, and you have determined your sign. The problem is that the Western transit point for the new year and the Chinese transit point for the new year are not the same. The Gregorian calendar regards January 1st as the transit point to a new year, whereas the transit point for the new year according to the Chinese solar calendar is February 4th.

In other words, if you are born before February 4th of any given year, you belong to the astrological sign of the previous year. If you were born after February 4th of a given year, then you belong to the astrological sign of that year.

Example 1: John was born on September 24, 1978. 1978 is the year of the Horse. Thus, John's Chinese astrology sign is the Horse.

Example 2: Rachel was born on February 3, 1982. Although 1982 is the year of the Dog, Rachel was born before the transit into the Dog year, which took place on February 4, 1982. Therefore, Rachel is considered to have been born in the year of the Rooster, the astrological sign for the previous year, and her Chinese astrology sign is that of the Rooster.

The animal signs of Chinese astrology

Dragon

Goat

Snake

Horse

Monkey

Dog

Ox

Pig

Tiger

Rooster

Rat

Rabbit

Combining feng shui with Chinese astrology personalizes your practice and creates rooms that not only look good, but empower your life.

Example 3: Michael was born on February 6, 1972. 1972 is the year of the Rat. As Michael was born after the transit point that marks the start of the year of the Rat, which is February 4, 1972, his astrological sign is that of the Rat. (The Chinese lunar new year fell on February 15, 1972. But because the Chinese lunar calendar is not used for astrology computations, the transit point of the lunar new year is not relevant to determining Michael's animal sign.)

Getting started

Now that you have a clear idea of the core theories and core basics, you're ready to move on to the practical side of classical feng shui. However, before you start putting the applications and techniques into practice, there are some basic preparatory activities that you need to undertake.

Many books neglect to show users exactly how to determine the various directional sectors of their home, in order to utilize flying stars or other classical feng shui techniques. If you don't know where the qi is exactly—which room, or even which corner—how do you know you're tapping into the right energies?

The basic preparatory activities of preparing a floor plan of your home, and marking out the nine palaces and the 24 Mountains, are an integral part of the process of getting real results from feng shui. That's what I'll be showing you how to do in the next chapter.

Chinese astrology: *more than just animal signs*

The Chinese have always had a profound curiosity about man's path in life, the journey of a person, and the question of who we are, why we are here, and what we are supposed to do during our brief time on this planet. This persistent curiosity about existential and metaphysical matters led the Chinese sages to develop methods for analyzing a person's destiny. These methods later evolved to become two separate systems of Chinese astrology, known as BaZi (Eight Characters, also known as Four Pillars) and Zi Wei Dou Shu (Purple Star astrology).

Chinese calligraphy, meaning "BaZi"

I prefer to use the term destiny analysis, because that is essentially the purpose of BaZi and Purple Star astrology in the modern world. Just as "biology is not destiny," so your astrology sign or destiny code should not entrap or limit you. Rather, it serves as a means by which you can be guided toward making better decisions and achieving your goals in life.

BaZi, in particular, is powerful and accurate with regard to life planning and unlocking your full potential. All aspects of your entire life—the pitfalls, trials, tribulations, and your wealth, status, personality, characteristics, talents, abilities, weaknesses, relationships—are all encoded within the eight characters, which are derived from your day and time of birth.

Chapter 2
Classical Feng Shui How-To's

In this chapter, I explain what you need to know and show you what to do before you can use the techniques in Part Two. These preparatory activities not only make it easy for you to apply the techniques, but also to make quick changes when your objectives alter. Like baking a cake, this chapter gives you the essential ingredients for feng shui success, from drawing your floor plan correctly to using a compass to discover the Facing direction of your home.

Before you begin this chapter

The techniques in Part Two will typically require you to do one of the following:

- Locate a room such as your bedroom or study in a specific sector of your home.
- Utilize a door located in a specific sector of your home to enter or exit your house (this, however, is limited just to houses, which may have more than one entrance).
- Place either a yang feature or a yin feature in a specific direction.

To apply the techniques successfully, you will need to know precisely which parts of your living space are located in which direction and in which sector. For example, you'll need to know where the north sector of your home is but also determine where, say, the east 2 direction is. In addition, you will need to know the natal flying stars chart of your property. This section shows you how to find this, and how to segment your home into the eight major directions and the 24 Mountains.

What you will need

- A floor plan of your home (see below).
- A compass or, if you can find one, a Chinese compass known as a Luo Pan.
- Colored pens and pencils, highlighters, and a ruler.

A note on floor plans

Using a professionally drawn floor plan will insure that you work to accurate dimensions. If you draw up a floor plan yourself, all the measurements should be accurate and the drawing to scale. Show the various rooms and partitions in your home, and the location of the entrances and doors, especially the main door. If your home has an irregular shape, square off any missing areas—see the diagram on page 59 as an example of how to do this.

Your natal flying stars chart

Finding the correct natal flying stars chart of your property is a two-step process. You will need to know:

- The Facing direction of the property.
- The period luck of the property.

The Facing direction

Finding the Facing direction of your property is done by standing at the Facing (the feng shui term for the orientation of the building) and then obtaining a direction from the compass or Luo Pan. As simple as it sounds, beginners are not the only ones who find this procedure quite challenging—finding the Facing can be perplexing for seasoned practitioners, too, because it is difficult with certain types of buildings.

All you need to begin to feng shui your home is a compass and a plan of each floor.

If the wrong Facing is used, then you will get a nasty domino effect. The wrong Facing direction results in the wrong flying stars chart being referenced. And the wrong flying stars chart will in turn result in zero—or, worse, bad—results, because the wrong qi is being activated!

Getting the Facing direction wrong is one of the most common mistakes made by beginners. It is also one of the main reasons why people don't see results when they try to utilize feng shui. It is a bit like being given incorrect driving directions to a destination—if you are lucky, you simply end up in the wrong place. If you are unlucky, you get completely lost and find yourself in the middle of nowhere!

In traditional Chinese houses, establishing the Facing of the building was never a problem. This is because traditional Chinese houses always had their main door in the facade of the building, which was also the Facing.

Modern homes are more creative, and mass-scale housing means doors are not always located at the front facade of the house. Apartments also present a unique challenge when finding the Facing, as some have confusing or multiple facades.

With some properties, the facade is often the definitive guide to the Facing. With others, determining the Facing is a cumulative exercise—you take into account all the factors, then make a judgment.

The Facing of a house

In almost 80 percent of houses, finding the Facing isn't a problem. The facade is usually obvious, and it is often very clear which way the house has been built to face. The key is to use the facade to determine the Facing. If there is no obvious facade or if it is not clear which road the building is facing, then you will need to use the location of the main door *and* the location of the busiest street, to determine the Facing.

The most common mistake that is made when it comes to finding the Facing of a house is to immediately assume that the main door is synonymous with the Facing of a building. Always assess the Facing independently from the main door's location, unless your facade is not immediately obvious.

In this home, the main door faces south, but the Facing of the building is eastablished as west because of the house's main facade; this direction also has the most yang activity owing to the main road.

The Facing of an apartment, loft, or condominium

In apartments, lofts, and condominiums, the Facing of the property can be a little harder to determine. Many modern constructions have sophisticated and sometimes deceptive or multiple facades. Increasingly, many high-rise buildings are built to afford all the apartments or units within the building a view, making it difficult to ascertain which way the building has been built to face.

As a general rule, always look first at the way the building appears to be oriented. Most of the time, by looking at the facade of the building or the direction in which it was built to face (usually a view of a park or the skyline) you will be able to ascertain its Facing.

Always regard architectural features like the main entrance or a lobby as supportive evidence only of the Facing. Imagine the building as a person—a person's eyes could be looking one way, but their entire body is facing another direction. Similarly, the main entrance or lobby of an apartment building is not definitive proof of the building's Facing.

Where the building has multiple or deceptive facades, where it is not obvious which way the building is built to face, or where the building is round, you will need to look at other factors. As a rule of thumb, where the building is round, its main entrance is usually the point of reference for the Facing. Where the building is not round, but has no obvious facade or orientation, look at where the main door is located and the side of the building that is most yang, or active and busy (typically, the side that faces a street, or that receives the most light).

Once you have the Facing of the building established, you can proceed to take the direction of the Facing, using the steps overleaf.

Establishing the Facing direction of an apartment building: what not to do

* Don't use the apartment or unit Facing to establish the Facing direction.
* Don't assume that the main entrance or lobby is always located at the Facing side of the building, and therefore take a direction from the lobby.
* Don't take the Facing direction from the balcony of the apartment or unit, or take the Facing direction from the entrance to the apartment complex.

When it comes to apartments, every unit within a block or building shares a common flying stars chart. This is because a block or building is regarded as one house, and each of the units is a room in the house. That is why we use the Facing of the entire building, not just the unit, to establish the Facing direction and, in turn, the flying stars chart.

Having a single flying stars chart for all the units in a building doesn't mean there are no differences in each unit. Remember, the door to each unit will be located in a different sector, depending on the location of the unit. That alone is enough to create a distinctly different quality of feng shui.

Step by step

Taking a direction using a compass

1 At the Facing of the building, stand in the center, with your back to the building or structure, looking out. Hold up your compass and wait for the needle to settle and steady at magnetic north. If the compass needle continually fluctuates and does not settle in any one direction, then it is possible that the door frame or the building is emanating a strong electromagnetic force that is disrupting the ability of the compass to orientate itself to the magnetic north. Take two steps forward or two steps back—this will usually move you out of the magnetic field of metal door frames or any metal structures. Establish the direction from there.

2 Discover the Facing direction of the building by looking up the compass reading on the chart opposite.

Step by step

Taking a direction using a Luo Pan

1 Stand in the center of the Facing, with your back to the building or structure, and looking out. Hold up your Luo Pan and wait for the needle to settle itself and steady.

2 Once the needle steadies itself, turn the Luo Pan's dial until the round end of the needle is aligned between the two red dots.

3 To determine the direction of the Facing, look at which sector the red string is aligned over—you will get a sector reading and a degree reading this way. You now have the Facing direction of the property.

Finding your home's Facing direction by compass reading

Here are ranges of compass readings and the Facing directions they relate to. When you have found your home's Facing, check to see which period it falls into (see page 52), and then refer to your home's natal chart on pages 76–81.

North 1	337.5°–352.5°
North 2/3	352.5°–22.5°
Northeast 1	22.5°–37.5°
Northeast 2/3	37.5–67.5°
East 1	67.5–82.5°
East 2/3	82.5–112.5°
Southeast 1	112.5–127.5°
Southeast 2/3	127.5–157.5°
South 1	157.5–172.5°
South 2/3	172.5–202.5°
Southwest 1	202.5–217.5°
Southwest 2/3	217.5–247.5°
West 1	247.5–262.5°
West 2/3	262.5–292.5°
Northwest 1	292.5–307.5°
Northwest 2/3	307.5–337.5°

Your main door usually identifies your home's Facing, but check other factors such as main roads and the house's facade first.

Period luck: the time factor

The Facing direction is one of the two factors that determine a building's flying stars chart. The other is the period luck of the building. In flying stars feng shui, qi moves in cycles of twenty years. Altogether, there are nine cycles or periods, each comprising twenty years. These periods are referenced by number: period 1, period 2, and so on. At the end of period 9, we return to period 1. Period luck is a sort of shorthand used by classical feng shui practitioners to identify the specific period of a building (similar to the way architecture is classified according to its historical period, such as Federal or Victorian). It is essentially a form of classification of the prevailing energies at the time the building was first occupied.

What does this mean on a practical level? Every twenty years, the flying stars chart for each of the 24 Mountains is different. Hence, a property facing south 2 that was first occupied prior to 2004, which is part of the period 7 cycle, will have an entirely different flying stars chart from a property facing south 2 that was first occupied in 2007, which is part of the period 8 cycle.

A useful analogy to help you understand this concept of different qi in different periods is to think about it within the context of power supply. A house built in 2004 would have been connected to the power grid and thus energized in 2004. A house built in 2007, however, would have been connected to the power grid and only energized in 2007. So at which point do we consider a building to have been "energized" or to have "begun its life" in the feng shui sense?

In classical feng shui, the move-in date is always used as the reference point for ascertaining the period of the property, and therefore the flying stars chart of the property. So, for example, two houses in the same row, constructed and completed at the same time, but first occupied at different times, could technically have different flying stars charts.

If the house is occupied, and then vacated, within the twenty years of a single luck period, the flying stars chart of the house does not change. But if the house is left vacant for more than six months, during which time there is a changeover to a new period (for example, between

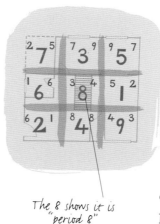

The 8 shows it is "period 8"

This home has a period 8 natal chart, as it was first occupied in 2005.

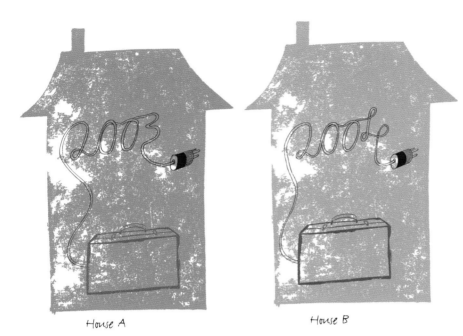

House A   House B

Two identical-looking homes can have different qi and therefore a different flying stars chart depending on when they are first occupied.

2003 and 2004, when the change from period 7 to period 8 took place), then the flying stars chart of the house will change. If the house remains continuously occupied by the same owner or family, but extensive renovations have been undertaken (such as changing the main door or installing a new roof or new floor tiles), then a period change can be deemed to have taken place.

Same house, different qi

For example, House A and House B (see illustration, above) are on the same row, and were occupied in 2003, which is period 7. House B was then sold by the owners and left vacant for more than a year. The new owners of House B moved into the house in 2004, which is period 8. So the owners of House B will have a period 8 chart. However, the occupants of House A, who have not moved, will continue to have a period 7 chart for their property.

With high-rise property, such as apartments, lofts, and condominiums, the situation is a little different. As already explained on page 47, an apartment building is treated as a single house, which means that the flying stars chart of the building, and correspondingly every apartment or unit in that building, is dictated by the flying stars chart of the building. Thus, typically, the point at which the *building* was first occupied is taken as the move-in date. It does not matter when the specific unit or apartment was occupied—what matters is when the building was first occupied.

For example, an apartment building is completed in 2003 but the first occupant only moves into the building in 2004. The flying stars chart of the building, and all the units within, is dictated by the move-in date of the first occupant, which is 2004, and it does not matter when the other occupants moved in.

Feng Shui Time Periods

Period	Duration
1	1864–1883
2	1884–1903
3	1904–1923
4	1924–1943
5	1944–1963
6	1964–1983
7	1984–2003
8	2004–2023
9	2024–2043

The nine periods

The table on the left shows you the nine periods of feng shui, consisting of twenty years per period, and the years that correspond to each of the nine twenty-year periods. The natal flying stars charts on pages 76–81 correspond to periods 6, 7, and 8, or the years 1964–2023.

Myth or truth?

The Compass school of feng shui versus the Forms school

Many books distinguish between different types of feng shui by classifying a system of feng shui as belonging to either the Compass school or the Forms school. This is a false distinction that is misleading and unhelpful.

All schools and systems of classical feng shui involve taking into consideration the land formations, or forms. All schools and systems of classical feng shui require a direction as the first point of reference, and as this can only be obtained using a compass or Luo Pan, all classical feng shui systems require the use of a compass or Luo Pan for the purposes of ascertaining directions. Accordingly, it is incorrect to separate classical feng shui systems into the Compass school or the Forms school.

Furthermore, there is no such name or concept in the classical texts on feng shui. If we are to distinguish between the two schools of thought in classical feng shui, the correct distinction is the Li Qi (or "theory of qi") school and Luan Tou (or "appearance of natural landforms") school.

Step by step

Finding your natal flying stars chart

1 If your home is an apartment building, the move-in date is the year in which the building was first occupied. If it is a house, the move-in date is the year in which you moved into and occupied the house.

2 Refer to the time periods table opposite and determine the correct period of the property.

3 Find the natal flying stars chart that corresponds to the Facing direction of the property, and the period of the property, using the reference charts on pages 76–81.

Example: the old apartment building

Sam has lived in an eight-story apartment building since 2004. The building, however, is an old one, and has been continuously occupied since 1980. Sam has found that his building faces southwest 3.

Although Sam has lived in the building since 2004, which is within period 8, the building has been occupied since 1980, which means the building is a period 6 building. Sam's apartment therefore will utilize the flying stars chart for a building facing southwest 3 in period 6.

Example: the house

Alice purchased a new single-story house in 2003 but moved into the property only in 2005. Her house faces east 2. As the move-in date into the property is 2005, Alice's house will utilize the flying stars chart for a building facing east 2 in period 8.

Example: the new apartment

Ryan purchased his apartment in 2002 while it was still under construction. The building was completed in 2003, and the first occupant moved in in that year. Ryan did not move into his apartment until 2005. This apartment faces southeast 3. Although Ryan moved in in 2005, the first occupant of the building moved in in 2003. Therefore, Ryan's apartment will utilize a period 7 chart rather than a period 8 chart.

Segmenting your home

Once you have the natal flying stars chart of your property, you have its qi map. All that remains is for you to ascertain which rooms or areas contain which stars, and which areas of your home fall within which directions in the 24 Mountains.

To do this segmenting of your home, we use two individual methods, which I call the nine palaces method and the pie chart method. Different techniques and applications that I'll show you will require you to reference the qi according to one or other of these.

In order to keep things simple, use two sets of floor plans, and label one as the nine palaces method, and the other as the pie chart method. That way, you can easily and quickly find the requisite room or the appropriate direction at a glance. For this section, you will need to have the following at hand:

- Natal flying stars chart for your property.
- Two copies of the floor plans of your property.
- Colored pens and a ruler.

Check what is considered part of your home, and what's not. If you have a small garden that takes the place of a missing sector or an integral garage you use, these areas are considered to be a part of your living space.

To garage or not to garage?

When we evaluate the feng shui of a property, the non-living space or areas that aren't enclosed, such as the garden, patio, or garage, are excluded from the evaluation. This is because these represent areas that are not living space as such. But if you worked in your garage, then it would be considered part of the living space.

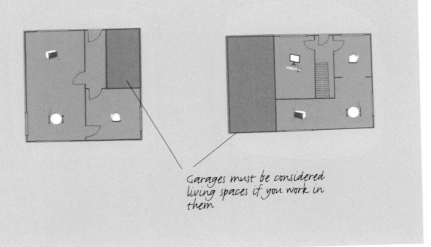

Garages must be considered living spaces if you work in them

The nine palaces method

This method divides up your property according to the nine palaces (sectors): one palace for each of the eight directions, plus one for the center of the property. The nine palaces method is integral to using the information from the flying stars chart of the property. This method helps you understand which stars reside in which parts of your property, enabling you to determine where to locate specific rooms, or which areas to utilize more (to tap into positive energies) and which to utilize less (to avoid the negative energies).

The two-thirds rule of missing palaces

L-shaped properties, and also properties that have slanted rooms or are rooms in which two of the walls are not parallel, will sometimes have a problem of missing corners. It may therefore be hard to decide if a palace is present or missing, so always use this two-thirds rule of thumb. If the area within the palace is more than two thirds of the palace, then the palace is considered present, but the qi is a little cramped. If only a small area of the palace is covered by a room or living space, and that area is less than two thirds of the palace, then the palace is officially missing.

The meaning of palace

The term "palace" is used in feng shui to describe different directional sectors of the home. It is a verbatim translation of the word Gong, which refers to the room or house where the qi is present. This is often added to the Gua associated with that direction, to form a single reference that encompasses not just the direction but also the type of energy or stars that could reside in that palace at a given time.

In feng shui it is common to mix the Chinese terms with the English ones, for brevity and ease of reference. So "Qian palace" refers to the northwest palace, while "Kun palace" refers to the southwest palace. (Both of these palaces are labeled in the annual flying stars chart shown on the left.) At the beginner stage, you can stick to using the directional terms (northwest palace, southwest palace, etc), and there's no need to worry about the Gua aspect yet.

SE	S	SW
4	9	2 Kun
3	5	7
8	1	6 Qian
NE	N	NW

E ... W

Each of the nine sectors has a Chinese name. "Gong" is the translation of "palace," so Qian would be known as Qian palace or Qian Gong.

Step by step

Superimposing the nine palaces grid and natal flying stars chart on a house floor plan

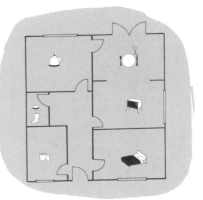

Begin with your floor plan, and square off any irregular areas.

1 Square off any irregular areas of your floor plan (see the box on page 59). Draw the nine palaces grid on your floor plan using a colored pen.

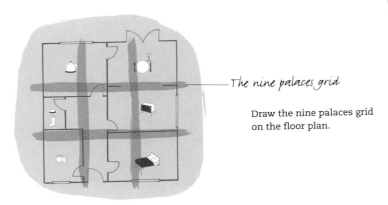

The nine palaces grid

Draw the nine palaces grid on the floor plan.

2 Establish where the Facing of your property is located on the floor plan. Place an arrow above the center grid box, pointing in the direction of your property's Facing. This is the house Facing direction.

3 Write down the Facing direction you obtained earlier (see page 45), in the center grid box of the Facing side of your property. For example, if your Facing direction is northwest, write northwest, or NW for short, in the center grid box.

4 You now have a reference direction. In sequence, mark the remaining seven directions within the remaining grid boxes.

5 Transfer the numbers from your home's flying stars chart onto the nine palaces grid.

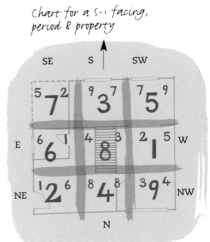

Chart for a S-1 facing, period 8 property

Step by step

Superimposing the nine palaces grid and natal flying stars chart on an apartment floor plan

As explained on page 47, when you are establishing the natal flying stars chart of an apartment, you use the natal flying stars chart of the entire building, because all the apartments in an apartment building share a universal flying stars chart. Thus, the Facing of the entire building is used to determine the Facing direction.

Apartment-dwellers need to use the flying stars chart for the whole building.

1 Draw the nine palaces grid on your apartment floor plan using a colored pen. (See the *Myth or truth?* box opposite for further guidance.) Find the central Tai Ji of your apartment (see page 62).

2 Stand in the center of your apartment and, using your compass, establish the location of the north sector.

3 Mark the north sector on your floor plan with the nine palaces grid.

4 You now have a reference direction. Mark the remaining seven directions within the remaining boxes of the grid.

5 Transfer the flying stars numbers from the natal chart to your floor plan.

Example: Jane lives in an apartment on the fifth floor of a ten-story building. First she draws the nine palaces grid on her apartment floor plan. She then establishes the central Tai Ji of her apartment by squaring off the floor plan and drawing two intersecting lines. Next, she stands in the center of her apartment and, using her compass, establishes the

Myth or truth?

Squaring off your floor plan... and the myth of the missing palaces

To square off your floor plan, draw dotted lines beyond any irregular areas (see right) until they intersect. Then you can find the central point of your home, or central Tai Ji when superimposing the pie chart on a floor plan (see page 62). If the missing area on your plan represents a third or more of the floor area, or a whole square of your home's flying stars grid, then you have a missing palace. In this case, you would need to extend the property to include the missing area. However, this situation is not common, and many homes have smaller missing palaces that won't cause a feng shui problem at all.

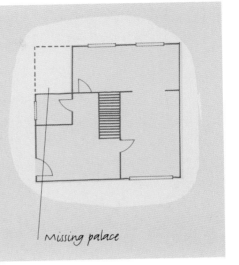

Missing palace

north direction. She ascertains that the north direction is located in the sector where her unit door (apartment main door) is located. On the floor plan, she marks the sector where her unit door is located as north. She then marks out the other seven directions accordingly. Finally, she transfers the flying stars numbers from the natal chart to her floor plan.

Differentiating Sitting and Facing

In feng shui, you will often hear references to the Sitting (Zuo) and the Facing (Xiang) of a building. What is the difference between these terms?

The Facing essentially refers to the direction in which the building faces. As explained on pages 45–6, this is not necessarily the front of the building, although usually the front of the building is the facade and therefore it corresponds to the Facing.

The Sitting refers to the direction in opposition to the Facing. For example, if a building has an east Facing, it will necessarily also have a west Sitting. In feng shui, we would say the building is "Facing east, Sitting west."

Feng shui shorthand for the Facing is usually an arrow, and for the Sitting it is usually an inverted arrow.

Use colored pens to help you distinguish between the three types of stars. Use one color for the Facing Star (top right), another for the Sitting Star (top left), and another for the Base Star (bottom).

Troubleshooting the nine palaces

Not all properties are created equal, and these days houses come in all shapes and sizes, and apartments may have funky designs. The rule is always to square off the property on the plan first, so that it is easy to draw the nine palaces on the map.

Once you have squared off the plan (see the box on page 59), then you can draw the nine palaces on it. It is important to be realistic when you draw them. If you have a missing palace, then you have a missing palace (see the two-thirds rule of missing palaces, page 56). There are no two ways about this.

Another common problem is how to deal with a property that is elongated either vertically or horizontally. Depending on which it is, you need to adjust the nine palaces accordingly. As a general rule, we don't like buildings that are very elongated, either vertically or horizontally, as this will result in cramped and squeezed qi.

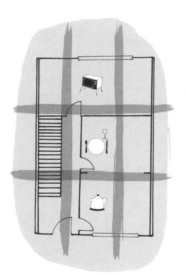

The nine palaces grid needs to echo the shape of an elongated dwelling.

A note about element cures

Classical feng shui regards cures as a last line of defense, employed only if there is really no other way to resolve the problem—it is still better to do something to try to negate or reduce the problem than to do nothing.

Where a cure is recommended, I give very specific options to insure that the cure you install is what I call a "pure element" cure. A pure element cure is actually rooted in the application of the five elements, rather than being a creative interpretation of the elements.

In the chart opposite are some broad guidelines to help you better understand how the cures I recommend in the subsequent chapters are derived. There is also advice on how to find appropriate substitutes if you cannot use the cures suggested.

Elements and their qualities

Element	Qualities

Fire

Needs to be a real fire to be a true Fire element cure. The fire must burn continuously or the flame has to be kept burning. However, this creates safety issues, so a red light (kept on continuously) can be used instead. Any item that produces heat, such as a portable heater, can also be used. As a very final resort, a red carpet or rug can be deployed. However, heaters (or any object that gives off heat) and red carpets or rugs are not considered "pure element" Fire cures and thus will be less effective.

Earth

Objects made from earth or stones will suffice for an Earth element cure. The key is to look for size or girth in the object, as Earth is supposed to be still and unmoving. If you are using a rock or earthenware sculpture, then make sure it is a reasonably large one. Obviously, pebbles would not make sense as they are too small.

Metal

Objects made from metal (brass, silver, gold, pewter, steel) will usually suffice for a Metal element cure, so long as the entire object is made from metal, or a large percentage of the object is metal. A wind chime is a popular feng shui metal cure—make sure, however, that the one you use has metal rods, not wooden or plastic tubing. Picture frames are too small to be real Metal cures. As a general rule, if you are using small objects such as brass cups, sports medals, or trophies, you need a good number of them for the element to have an effect. The bigger the room, the larger the item (or the greater the number of items) needs to be.

Water

Water cures are probably the easiest to implement because all you need is an open container filled with water—a large urn or bucket filled with water would do if you live in a small place. You need about 27 cubic feet (2.8 cubic meters) of water per 1,000 square feet (93 square meters) of space. However, if you are just implementing the cure for a room, then a container that will hold 3 quarts (3 liters) of water will probably suffice. The key is to keep the water clean, insure that it is exposed (ie, you can see the water's surface) to allow qi to collect, and, if you can, keep the water moving using an aeration pump or some fish.

Wood

Wood element cures are hard to implement indoors because the Wood must be live wood, in order to qualify for a wood cure. Live wood usually is a reference to real, living plants. When it comes to Wood cures, leafy plants are best, and preferably they should be planted in the ground or in a pot with soil.

The pie chart method

The second method for segmenting your home (see page 55) is the pie chart method, which is used to divide up the property into the 24 Mountains. This method is essential for determining which parts of your home fall within which direction. The 24 Mountains (see page 33) are primarily used for the placement of water features to activate specific types of stars such as Nobleman or Peach Blossom Stars.

They are also used to analyze "external" feng shui, but as that is beyond the scope of this book, I will not delve too much into it. This is because the placement of water features utilizing San He methods typically requires a higher level of precision, to pinpoint the area that falls within 15 degrees of a specific direction.

> *"The 24 Mountains are primarily used for the placement of water features"*

Step by step

Superimposing the pie chart on a floor plan

Use a fresh copy of your floor plan to do this.

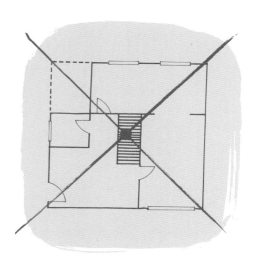

The central Tai Ji, or central point.

1   Establish the central Tai Ji of your house or apartment. The central Tai Ji is the point regarded as the actual center of any room or building. Finding the central Tai Ji is particularly important for an apartment, as this is how you determine north, which is used as a reference direction to establish the eight directions. To find the central Tai Ji, you first need to square off the room, building, or apartment (see the box on page 59). Now draw two intersecting lines from the upper right corner to the lower left corner, and from the upper left corner to the lower right corner. The meeting point of the two lines is the central Tai Ji. This is where you stand to establish the reference direction of north.

2   Stand at the central Tai Ji of your house or apartment. Using the compass, find the north direction, which is 0 degrees. Mark this approximately on your floor plan.

3   Mark the eight directions (north, south, east, west, northeast, northwest, southeast, southwest) on your floor plan, using a colored pen and a ruler.

4   Label the eight directions accordingly, using the alphanumeric shorthand for directions (such as SW2, N1).

5   Subdivide the eight directions into the 24 directions. It's a good idea to draw the lines a little beyond the boundaries of your house, in case you want to place water outside your home, in a particular sector.

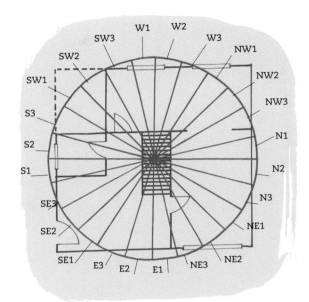

Begin by labeling the eight directions, then add in the others to give all 24 Mountains.

Ready to feng shui?

At this point, you should have on hand the following:

- One copy of your property floor plan, with the property's natal flying stars chart map superimposed on the nine palaces, and the eight directions (south, north, etc.) marked for easy reference.

- One copy of your property floor plan, with the 24 Mountains marked for easy reference.

At a glance, you should be able to identify the flying stars in each of the rooms in your property. You should also, at a glance, be able to determine which areas of your home fall within each of the 24 Mountains. You're now set to start putting classical feng shui to work for you, to support your endeavors and help you achieve your goals.

Chapter 3
Wealth Feng Shui—not just Money, Money, Money

There is a great misconception that feng shui is all about money and getting rich. While feng shui can be used to help you with matters of wealth, money is not the root of all feng shui. Before you can enhance your wealth, it's important to understand that in feng shui, wealth is defined in broader terms as prosperity—so practicing feng shui will help your health and relationships prosper along with your finances.

You say money, feng shui says prosperity

In classical feng shui, there is actually no reference to money as such. It does not speak of wealth, options trading, the stock market, or bullion. Classical feng shui texts do not contain advice on how to get rich. There is no secret Water Dragon formula or potent good-luck trinket that will instantly make you so wealthy that you never need to work again.

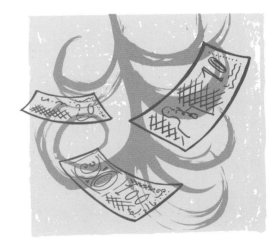

In pure, or classical, feng shui, wealth means prosperity, or good relationships and financial wealth.

Instead, in classical feng shui texts many of the techniques and ideas relate to achieving *prosperity*. In a modern context, people often associate prosperity with wealth, but that is not truly what it means. The word prosper means to thrive—which involves more than just being wealthy. Yes, it does mean to have money, but it also means to have good relationships with those around you and with those who matter. It means to have good health, to be emotionally, psychologically, and mentally contented, and to be happy, waking up every day thinking, "life is great!"

So, the goal of classical feng shui has always been to locate the individual in an environment that is comfortable, restful, rejuvenating, and energizing—an environment that promotes peace of mind, health, and comfort—leading to a more alert, effective, and productive individual.

When you are at the top of your game, feeling good about yourself and mentally geared for success, then you can identify opportunities, capitalize on them, and fulfill your true potential. This in turn leads to financial achievement and wealth.

It is, of course, silly to think that money is not important. There are very few people who do not aspire to great wealth. Most of us, at the very least, would like to achieve that holy grail of personal finance: being comfortable without having to work!

Classical feng shui can be applied to help you with your financial situation, whether it is to make more money or to resolve other kinds of money-related problems. But it is important to understand that classical feng shui is not a one-stop solution to all your financial woes or dreams. I'm not going to give you false hopes by suggesting that all you have to do is activate certain stars in your house and you'll be set for life.

You will still actually have to make an effort—going to work, spending time understanding your investments, or making sure your business has a viable business model. No matter how amazing your feng shui is, it is only 33 percent of the equation. Your own effort (or man luck) and your destiny (or heaven luck) need to be taken into account.

Get with the wang qi

In classical feng shui, there is no such thing as a universal wealth corner. There is a wealth sector in each home, but it is not universal. The wealth sector is actually a little different for each property.

Also, since the concept of wealth doesn't exist in classical feng shui texts, the term wealth sector is slightly inaccurate. It's more accurate to call it the vibrant qi sector. This is because in classical feng shui the way to acquire prosperity is through the use of vibrant qi, or wang qi in Chinese. This is essentially the positive, energizing qi that makes people happy, alert, and active. It is also the strongest qi of a particular period. Tapping into the vibrant qi, or wang qi, of your home simply involves more use of the areas where this type of qi is located or activating the vibrant qi using an object or element.

Where, then, did the term wealth sector come from? It most likely stems from feng shui practitioners engaging in some simplification for the sake of convenience. To make things easier for the clients, or simply to encourage people to utilize the area more, they simply labeled the vibrant qi areas wealth sectors.

Myth or truth?

Money and destiny

Making more money and having more wealth opportunities are not just a case of fixing your feng shui. Your personal destiny code (see page 41) comes into the equation as well. Feng shui cannot give you what you do not have in the first place. So you may need to realign or moderate your goals, adjust your perspective, change your attitude, and see how feng shui can help you, within the path that destiny has laid out for you. Sometimes that means adjusting the timing of your plans, being willing to take on certain challenges, or even being prepared for hardship. Being rich involves having the capacity to make money and keep it long enough to enjoy it. Even where people have the capacity and destiny for great wealth, that does not guarantee that they will actually become rich or fulfill their destiny.

The five grades of qi

All qi is not created equal and the idea behind the different grades of qi is to identify the quality of the qi (benevolent or malevolent) and also its maturity or timeliness, which tells us if the qi is strong or weak. Qi can be graded into five stages: killing qi (sha qi), dead qi (si qi), retreating qi (tui qi), growing qi (sheng qi), and vibrant qi (wang qi).

On a simplistic level, we want always to make use of qi that is benevolent and strong and avoid the qi that is malevolent and weak. Thus, we prefer to tap into either growth qi or vibrant qi, and stay away from the killing qi, dead qi, or retreating qi.

Here is a table that may give you some idea of how the qi ranks:

Qi	Stage	Description
Wang qi	Vibrant (prosperous)	Full of life, represents present wealth, current happiness and fulfillment
Sheng qi	Growing (growth)	Up-and-coming, future wealth, future gains
Tui qi	Retreating	Slowing down, lethargic, fickle
Si qi	Dead	Stagnation, not progressive
Sha qi	Killing (aggressive)	Aggressive, volatile and destructive, causes harm

It is important to use technically precise terminology when we discuss qi because it comes in different grades. In a property, qi is graded according to its timeliness or maturity (yes, a bit like cheese and wine) and whether it is benevolent or malevolent in nature. And in most matters, but especially wealth matters, we want to use the right grade of qi. Specifically, we want to use the most mature form, which is vibrant qi (wang qi), and the second-most mature form, which is growth qi (sheng qi).

Because the term wealth sector is quite predominant in the feng shui vocabulary of most people, even beginners to the subject, I'll continue to use the term—so let's track down those wealth sectors.

Locating the wealth sectors in your home

Every home has wealth qi that can be activated—and I speak from my experience as a classical feng shui practitioner, having seen homes of all shapes and sizes. Unless you are living on a boat, in a tree house, or under a freeway, you can activate and tap into the wealth qi in your property. It is just a matter of knowing where the wealth sectors are and how to access the wealth qi located there.

The key lies in the fact that the wealth sectors are always related to the location of the Wealth Stars of a given luck period (for example, period 8). There are three Wealth Stars in any property that can be activated and used to gain benefits of a financial nature. In any given period, there is always one Main Wealth Star, and two Secondary Wealth Stars. The Main Wealth Star corresponds to the vibrant qi of the period, because vibrant qi relates to current cash flow or income that is currently being received. The two Secondary Wealth Stars correspond to the growing qi of the period, because growing qi relates to future cash flow or income that is invested.

All you have to do is know which stars are the prevailing three Wealth Stars for the current period, locate them in your home, and activate them. It's that simple.

During period 8, which spans 2004–2023, the Main Wealth Star is the #8 Star (also known as the 8 White Star), specifically the #8 Facing Star. Wherever the #8 Facing Star is located in your home, that is the location of the vibrant qi sector for period 8.

The two Secondary Wealth Stars for period 8 are the #9 and #1 Stars. Wherever the #9 and #1 Facing Stars are located in your home, that is the location of the growing qi sector(s) for period 8.

I dream of money

As a general rule, a feng shui consultant will usually prefer to utilize the main door or an activity room (such as a television room, family room, home office, study, or workroom) to tap into the benefits of the Wealth Stars. Although it is not wrong to sleep in a room with Wealth Stars, this generally results in a poorer quality of sleep.

If you sleep in a bedroom where the #8 Facing Star or the annual #8 Star is located, you will probably have difficulty getting a good night's sleep. This is largely because you won't be able to switch off your mind, as it will be constantly occupied with thoughts about work. However, this only applies to the #8 Stars and is less of a problem with the #9 and #1 Stars, because their qi is not so strong and active.

Step by step

Finding the Wealth Stars in your home

If you have done the basic preparatory activities outlined in Chapter 2, you should have with you one copy of your home's floor plan with the nine palaces grid and with the natal flying stars chart superimposed on the floor plan, and one copy of your home's floor plan with the 24 directions marked using the pie chart method. To find the Wealth Stars in your home, you will need only to use the floor plan with the flying stars chart superimposed on it.

Locate the #8, 9, and 1 Facing Stars on the floor plan to find your wealth hot-spots.

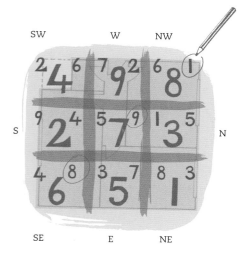

1   Using a red pen, locate the #8 Facing Star in the floor plan. Remember, the Facing Star is always the star on the top right-hand corner of each grid box. Circle the #8 Facing Star with a red pen. You've now found the location of the Main Wealth Star in your home.

2   Locate the #9 and #1 Facing Stars in the floor plan, and circle them with your red pen. You've now found the two Secondary Wealth Star locations in your home—and have located your home's wealth sectors.

Activating the Wealth Stars

Having now found the Wealth Stars in your home, you are probably itching to activate their wealth qi, but there is one more thing to do first. Because feng shui is a goal-orientated practice, you must first give some thought to the nature of the wealth-related problem that you are facing. To use a medical analogy, a diagnosis is needed before a prescription can be given.

In classical feng shui, there is no one-size-fits-all solution. Everything depends on the nature of your problem and on your needs. Financial issues vary greatly and the solution isn't always just to facilitate making more money. So, sit down and give some thought to the nature of the problem. For example, are you making good money from your job but are somehow constantly in debt? Or is it a case of not making enough

Wealth and the time factor

In classical feng shui nothing is forever. Qi is dynamic, so its quality keeps changing with the passage of time. Each period has its own Main and Secondary Wealth Stars. The Main Wealth Star and Secondary Wealth Stars for period 8, for example, will not be the same as those for period 7 or for period 9.

PERIOD	FACING STARS	
	Main Wealth Star	Secondary Wealth Star
7 (1984–2003)	7	8, 9
8 (2004–2023)	8	9, 1
9 (2024–2043)	9	1, 2
1 (2044–2063)	1	2, 3

However, there is always an element of continuity, as you can see from the chart. Secondary Wealth Stars are the connecting bridge between two consecutive periods. This is because one of the Secondary Wealth Stars in any given period is always the Main Wealth Star for the period that follows. For example, the #8 Star, which was one of the Secondary Wealth Stars for period 7, becomes the Main Wealth Star for period 8.

Secondary Wealth Stars are sometimes referred to as Future Wealth Stars because they are in the process of maturing and becoming stronger. When the period changes and these stars reach the peak of the energy cycle, they become the prevailing, most powerful energies for that given time. Hence, it is essential to move with the energies and keep up with the qi!

At present, we are in period 8, which runs from 2004 to 2023. The Main Wealth Star in period 8 is the #8 Facing Star. The Secondary Wealth Stars in period 8 are the #9 and #1 Facing Stars. For now, just look for these three stars in your home.

When we transit over to period 9, which runs from 2024 to 2043, the Main Wealth Star will become the #9 Facing Star, which will have matured and will be the most powerful star of the period. The qi of the #8 Facing Star will be diminished and expiring. The Secondary Wealth Stars in turn will be the #1 and #2 Facing Stars.

money or barely making ends meet? Perhaps you are financially comfortable, but would like to be able to reach the next level by having a bit more money to invest or spend. Or are you financially comfortable but seemingly unable to grow your money through investments?

Take a look at the checklist on page 73 setting out possible financial problems and put a tick next to the problems you think you are facing. Be honest with yourself. You may need to take out your financial statements and have a long, hard look at them before deciding the nature of your problem. It's also important to consider if your goals are short-term (perhaps one month, six months, or one year) or long-term in nature (say, five, ten, or twenty years).

Once you've identified the nature of your problem, it's time to look at how to solve your problem. The checklist shows you the appropriate

Before you begin to feng shui for wealth, clarify your objectives. Then locate the stars in the key rooms of your home.

section in this chapter that you should turn to, to learn what you can do to resolve your problem using classical feng shui techniques.

It is possible that you may have more than one problem at a time. For example, maybe you have debt and are also having difficulty with the income from your job. Always solve the most immediate problem first, and then move on to the other problem.

Problem

- My finances are sound but I would like to make a little extra in the next few months to afford a one-off purchase.

- My finances are sound but I would like to make a little extra so that I can afford to buy a new car or my own apartment.

- My finances are sound but I don't seem to have much luck with investments.

- I am a salaried employee. I make good money now but would like my job to pay me more.

- I am self-employed. I make good money now but would like to make more.

- I have short-term credit card debts—I overspent last month.

- I have recent credit card debt or a recent debt problem—I've never had this problem before.

- I've just spent quite a lot on a vacation or expensive purchase and want to be able to recoup some of that money.

- I have always been able to save money, but lately it seems that expenses have gone up and I just don't know where my money goes.

- I have a serious credit card debt—I can't keep up with repayments (it's the story of my life).

- I have serious debts (credit card, mortgage, car repayment, student loan) despite having a good job. The debt just keeps piling up.

- I have a good job which pays me a good income, but I don't know where the money goes and can't seem to save much.

Solution

See "Using the annual flying stars for a short-term increase in wealth opportunities" (page 101).

See "Activating the #8 Facing Star for wealth opportunities" (page 82).

See "Activating the #9 and #1 Facing Stars for investment opportunities" (page 88).

See "Activating the #8 Facing Star for wealth opportunities" (page 82).

See "Activating the #9 and #1 Facing Stars for investment opportunities" (page 88).

See "Using the annual flying stars for a short-term shortage of wealth problem" (page 97).

See "Using the annual flying stars for a short-term shortage of wealth problem" (page 97).

See "Using the annual flying stars for a short-term increase in wealth opportunities" (page 101).

See "Using the annual flying stars for a short-term shortage of wealth problem" (page 97).

See "Handling the #3 and #5 Stars" (page 91).

See "Handling the #3 and #5 Stars" (page 91).

See "Handling the #3 and #5 Stars" (page 91).

Using the natal flying stars chart or the annual stars

In the following pages, you will find specific classical feng shui solutions for the clutch of problems that I have highlighted. The first section focuses on problems that can be resolved using the natal flying stars chart of the property. The second section focuses on problems that can be resolved using the annual flying stars chart. You might now be wondering what the difference is between the two.

The natal flying stars chart is the flying stars chart of your home. It is unique to your property and your property alone, as it is based on the Facing direction and period luck of your property. For example, the palace location of the #8 Facing Star in your home, and that of your friend who lives, say, in the next street, will not necessarily be the same. By contrast, the annual flying stars chart is uniform for everyone. So the palace location of the #8 Star will be the same for everyone in any given year, irrespective of the Facing direction of the home.

The natal flying stars chart is generally used for a fundamental problem of a long-term nature. For example, if you have persistently been unable to save money or never seem to make enough, then it's a long-term, fundamental problem. When you use the natal flying stars chart, you are looking to achieve your results over a prolonged period of time, say anywhere upward of two to ten years.

In contrast, the annual flying stars chart is used for quickie fixes. It is for temporary or short-term wealth-related problems such as melting your credit card at a crazy sale or on a one-off indulgence, or paying for the vacation of a lifetime.

A really easy way to distinguish between the natal flying stars chart and the annual flying stars chart is to look at the numbers present in each grid box. A natal flying stars chart will show three stars in each box: a Base Star, a Sitting Star, and a Facing Star. An annual flying stars chart will only show one star—a Base Star—in each grid box. At this basic level, each chart can be used independently.

Annual flying stars chart

Natal flying stars chart

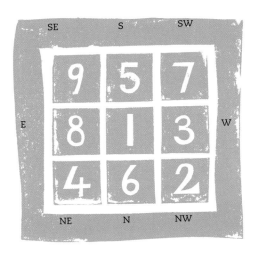

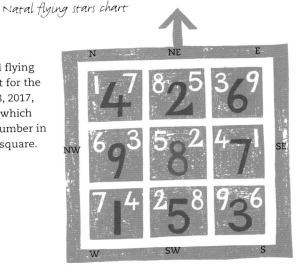

An annual flying stars chart for the years 2008, 2017, and 2026, which has one number in each grid square.

A period 8 chart, which also features Facing and Sitting stars, or numbers. This chart is for a NE2/3 property.

To avoid confusion and complexity, keep in mind your objective:

- If it is a *short-term* objective, then always look at the annual flying stars chart, and ignore or put aside the natal flying stars chart. Focus on using the right annual flying stars chart areas, even if those areas are unfavorable or negative in the natal flying stars chart. So, for example, if you want to use the annual #8 Star for Wealth, even if it is located in a part of your home which has no favorable stars based on the natal flying stars, use that area for the year.

- If it is a *long-term* objective, then ignore the annual flying stars chart and go for the natal flying stars chart.

At the basic level, you need to keep your focus clear and not be blinded by too much information. Focus on your goals and use the right stars, and you'll have your solution.

Natal flying stars charts for period 6

Here are the 16 natal charts for feng shui period 6, which runs from 1964 through 1983.

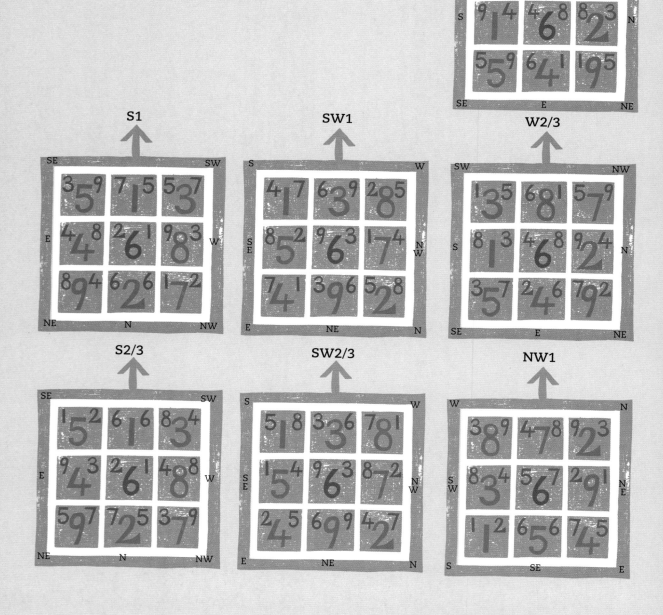

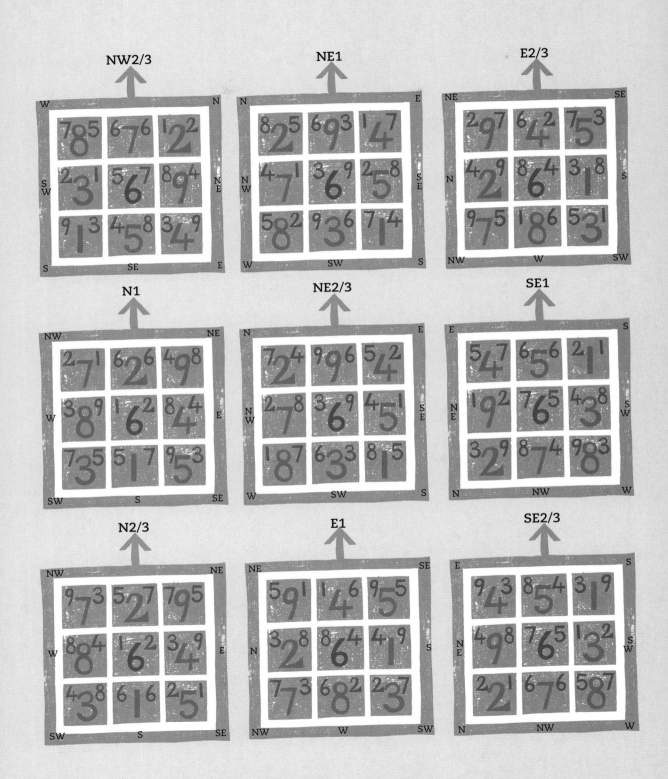

Natal flying stars charts for period 7

Here are the 16 natal charts for feng shui period 7, which runs from 1984 through 2003.

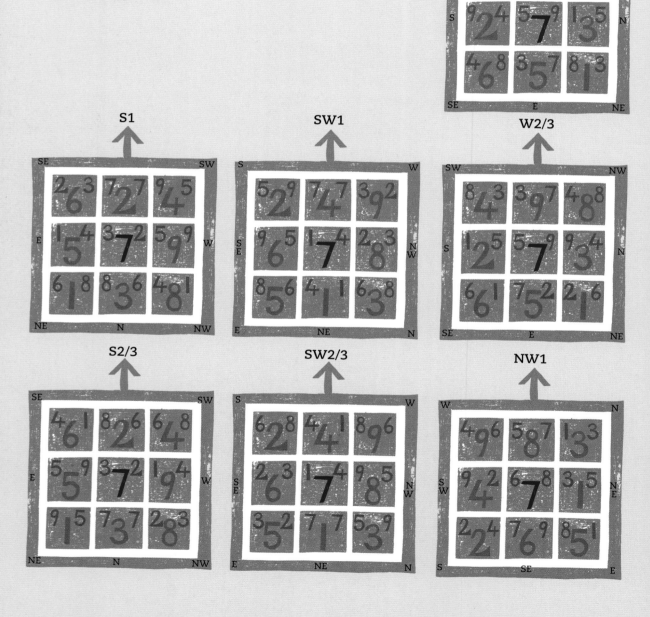

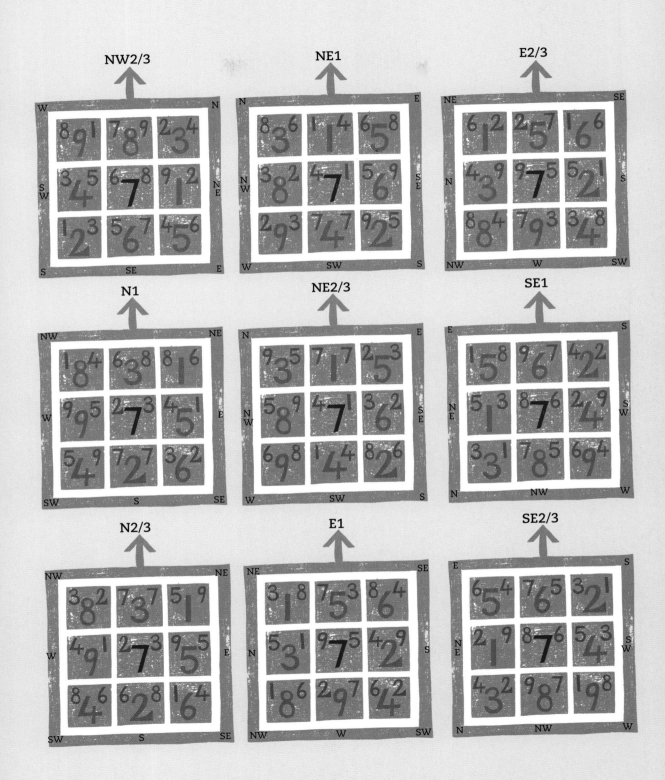

Natal flying stars charts for period 8

Here are the 16 natal charts for feng shui period 8, which runs from 2004 through 2023.

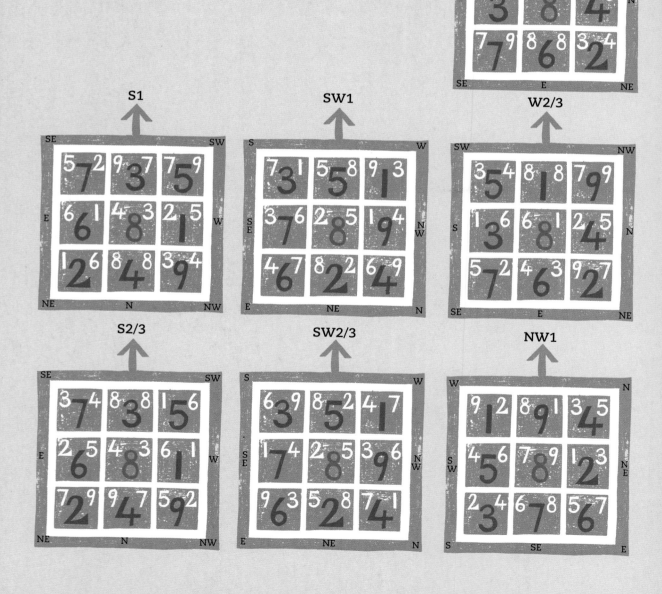

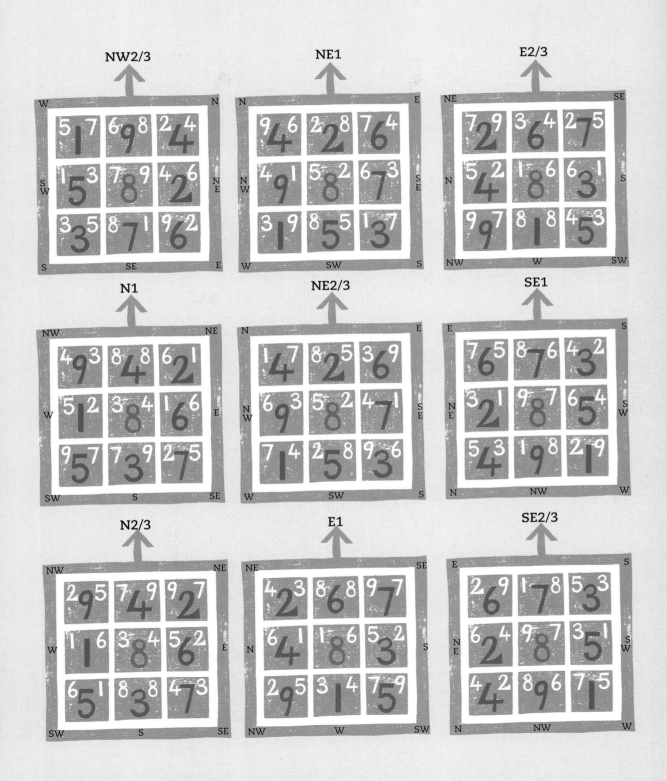

Resolving long-term and fundamental wealth problems using the natal flying stars chart

How do you know if your wealth problem is fundamental and long-term in nature? Easy. If the wealth problem is persistent, then it is likely to be fundamental and long-term in nature. If year after year you find yourself looking at a bank account that is rarely black and mostly red, or if you consistently find yourself unable to pay the rent or your bills, you have a persistent wealth problem.

"If you consistently find yourself unable to pay the rent or your bills, you have a persistent wealth problem"

It is important to be honest with yourself at this stage. At the same time, it is also vital to recognize that your present difficulty may have more than just one cause. Do not be discouraged, however—resolving your problem is possible. You just need a little patience, and to take things step by step.

The way to use this section is simple: use the checklist on page 73 to pinpoint what your problem is, and then implement the solutions suggested. As you will be using the natal flying stars chart, the outcomes will not be as fast as if you were using the annual flying stars chart, but you want to solve a fundamental problem using a long-term solution, not a short-term one. Natal flying stars do not work quickly, but their effects are more prolonged and sustained in the long run.

Activating the #8 Facing Star for wealth opportunities

● *My finances are sound but I would like to make a little extra so that I can afford to buy a new car or my own apartment.*

● *I am a salaried employee. I make good money now but would like my job to pay me more.*

If you are in either of the above situations, activating the #8 Facing Star will bring about consistent, long-term improvements to your finances.

The most obvious outcome you can expect from activating the #8 Facing Star is a pay raise or better perks in your present job, or opportunities to move to a job with better pay. If you are in the wheeling and dealing line (such as in sales or business development), you can expect bigger, juicier deals to come your way. If you are in a creative field, you will have opportunities to undertake lucrative but also challenging and interesting projects. If you are an entrepreneur or a business owner, using the #8 Facing Star will not just enable you to land bigger deals but will mean that any money owing to you is collected without too much difficulty.

You can activate wealth and prosperity simply by using a room inhabited by Wealth Stars as a workroom or home office.

Most importantly, your job will feel like less of a grind. You will have a greater sense of fulfillment when you work, and, of course, those job satisfaction levels will definitely go up.

There are four main ways in which you can make use of the #8 Facing Star:

- Locate the main door in the #8 Facing Star.
- Use the room (or the area if there isn't a room) where the #8 Facing Star is located as a workroom, study, or home office.
- Place an aquarium at the #8 Facing Star.
- Place an active object such as a television, air conditioner, fan, or hi-fi in this room.

An aquarium activates the #8 Facing Star.

Let me elaborate a little on each of these techniques, so you can understand the rationale behind them.

Locating the main door in the #8 Facing Star

The main door, defined as the door that you use to enter your home, is considered a yang feature. This is because it is an activity area—think of how many times you go in and out in a day. With each time you enter and exit the home, you are activating the qi by moving it and circulating it. This is all the more so if you live with your family and many people are coming and going at all hours of the day.

In classical feng shui, the main door is known as the qi mouth of the house, because it is the main point where qi enters the property for circulation. When the qi mouth of the house is located at the #8 Facing Star, then the house is considered to be already receiving positive qi from the Wealth Star of the period.

If your main door is located in the same sector as the #8 Facing Star, you already are activating the #8 Facing Star and there's nothing more you need to do, except to make sure that the area is uncluttered, broad, and well lit. You may also want to insure that some of the basic rules on main door forms are observed (see Door rules, opposite).

No door? Use the window

If you have no main door where the #8 Facing Star is located, but you do have a window in that area, open the window regularly. This will allow the vibrant qi in the area to circulate. You won't get the same level of benefits as from using a main door in that area, but it's better than nothing. Don't let what you can't do stop you from doing what you can do.

Door rules

As the main door is the qi mouth of the home, and the main entrance point for qi from the external environment, it needs not only to be located in the right place, but also to have the right forms, internally and externally. "Forms" is the shorthand for landforms, or luan tou.

Externally, the term refers to land contours, mountains, and environmental features, which can have an impact upon the qi flow and movement. Forms also include man-made objects such as telephone poles, lampposts, and sharp roofs of neighboring homes.

Internal forms encompass contours and features within the home such as overhead beams and sharp corners. Ideally, we want a property to have not only good external forms, but also good internal forms.

As regards the main door of a home, certain features will compromise the quality of the qi that enters your home or, worse, entirely block the qi from coming into your home. Try to avoid all of the following:

- Beams running across or over the main door area.
- A tight area internally and externally around the main door (the area just outside the main door, and just inside in the foyer area, should be spacious, open, and lit by natural light if possible).
- A sharp corner pointing at the main door.
- A lamppost, telephone pole, or tree in front of the main door.
- A dark, shaded main door area caused by trees or dense foliage.

If your house has multiple entrances, and one of those entrances is located in the sector where the #8 Facing Star is located, then you should try to utilize that door more often to enter and exit your house.

Design constraints may make it difficult for you to locate a door or entrance at the #8 Facing Star. Apartments usually have this problem because there is almost always only one door to enter and exit. In that case, try one of the following alternatives.

Using the room or area in the #8 Facing Star for work

The next best thing to having a main door at the #8 Facing Star is utilizing the room where the star is located for work-related activities. In other words, if you can't put a door where the star is, then put your work there, to tap into the star's energies. After all, money is made most of the time through work—by working in the #8 Facing Star room or area, you are already activating the star because work is a yang activity. Directly tapping into the positive energies of the #8 Facing Star will assist you in endeavors and actions that are directly linked to the generation of wealth.

All you have to do is look at the floor plan of your home that has the flying starts chart on it (see pages 56–60) and locate the #8 Facing Star. Can that room or area become a work space? If you are currently using it for something else, such as a spare bedroom, is it possible for it to double as your home office or workspace? Or, if the #8 Facing Star is located in the dining room, say, perhaps you could utilize a laptop to work in there.

This strategy is particularly helpful if you work at least part-time from home or if you run your own business from a home office. If you are a writer or an artist, it will make you more productive (we all know about those artistic tendencies to take coffee breaks while awaiting the arrival of the muse). You will be able to focus better, will have a more optimistic outlook about your career, and, best of all, will have a torrent of ideas to keep you busy.

If you wish to bring in your personal favorable directions, which are derived from your Gua number (see page 32), you can try to align your work desk so that it faces your personal sheng qi or yan nian directions.

Study rules

If you are planning to locate your study, workroom, or home office at the #8 Facing Star, you are taking an important step toward improving your wealth opportunities and improving your financial position in life. However, it is important that rules on internal forms are also observed. If the internal forms are negative in the room, then you will find that the quality of the qi in that room is compromised, if not negated. Accordingly, it is always important to check the forms first before using the room.

If the room has any of the following negative features, it is unsuitable for use as a study, workroom, or home office and you won't be able to get many benefits from the #8 Facing Star, because the qi is compromised by the forms. These negative features include:

• A dark, small and windowless room.
• Slanting, uneven, or low ceilings.
• Beams running crisscross overhead.
• An awkwardly shaped room (particularly common in attic rooms or small cottages).
• Awkward corners in the room making it difficult to position a desk squarely.

As a general rule, always position your desk so that it is not located under any visible beams or you will find it difficult to concentrate when working. It is also important not to position your back to the door, as this results in the qi that enters your room striking your back. If you wish, you can try to position your desk so that it faces one of your personal favorable directions (see page 32), provided you don't breach the forms rules listed above.

If you are not familiar with these, don't worry—opt instead to make sure that you have good internal forms in the room as well (see Study rules, opposite).

Outcomes will, of course, vary from property to property, because there is the additional factor of external landforms to take into account (see page 85). This aspect will influence the extent to which the qi of the area is optimized. However, you should see improvements within four to six months of beginning to use the area where the #8 Facing Star is located, as long as you do not have an issue with the internal forms.

Placing an aquarium in the #8 Facing Star

If you cannot place your work area in the #8 Facing Star, all is not lost. You can still activate the #8 Facing Star by placing an aquarium in the room where it resides. The star is activated by yang activities, and Water is regarded as a yang element in classical feng shui. By placing the Water in the #8 Facing Star location, you are activating the qi in that area with the active Water.

Unfortunately, this technique is not usable in every situation. If the #8 Facing Star is located in the west, northwest, northeast, or south palace of your property, then you cannot place Water in these locations. You will need to utilize an active object to activate the #8 Facing Star (see Placing an active object in the #8 Facing Star, page 88).

An aquarium can be placed in any room where the #8 Facing Star resides in order to activate wealth.

External Water versus internal Water: An aquarium is regarded in classical feng shui as internal Water. While this is a good way to activate the #8 Facing Star, in classical feng shui natural water formations, specifically external Water, are always considered superior to man-made internal Water. External Water refers to natural bodies of water such as ponds, lakes, creeks, and rivers. Accordingly, if you have natural water outside the palace where the #8 Facing Star resides and if it is in a palace where Water can be located, this is considered superior to placing an aquarium or water feature in the palace where the #8 Facing Star is located.

Turn on your #8 Wealth Stars by turning on a television or fan placed where the #8 Star resides.

Placing an active object in the #8 Facing Star

Televisions, air conditioners, fans, and hi-fi's are regarded as moving, or active, objects and so are regarded as having a yang quality. Accordingly, they are often used to activate the #8 Facing Star when it is located in a palace that is not suitable for the placement of Water. If it is located in the west, northwest, northeast, or south palace, you cannot activate the #8 Facing Star using an aquarium or water feature, and instead will have to use a television, air conditioner, fan, or hi-fi.

Obviously, merely installing these devices in the room is not going to move the qi. In order for the qi to move and be active, the room must be well used—it could be a television room, for example, or an activity area where family and friends can socialize, play cards, or watch movies. The more you use the room and employ these yang devices, the more you will activate and move the qi in the room.

There is no need to make sure the television or hi-fi faces your Personal Favorable Directions (see page 32)—you're not using it to work but to relax. Just make sure the room is not cluttered (don't cram too much furniture or equipment into it) and open the windows periodically to let the qi circulate. Make sure the room is brightly lit, ideally in the form of natural sunlight during the day.

Activating the #9 and #1 Facing Stars for investment opportunities

● *My finances are sound but I don't seem to have much luck with investments.*

● *I am self-employed. I make good money now but would like to make more.*

In either of the above situations, activating the #9 or #1 Facing Star will create or improve opportunities to make good investments or to sell an existing investment favorably. As the #9 and #1 Facing Stars are the Future Wealth Stars, they are used to improve long-term wealth opportunities. They will not produce immediate financial benefits like a pay raise or a chance to move to a better-paying job. Instead, you will find that they bring about less tangible financial benefits—for example, turning around a non-performing investment (such as a property you cannot sell or rent out).

You have to be a bit careful when determining how to handle the #9 and #1 Facing Stars in your property. If, for example, you have no investments at all, then activating these stars will help you find good opportunities for investment or enable you to utilize your skills to create intellectual property from which you can generate income.

On the other hand, if you have made investments but have not had much luck with them (for example, perhaps you often lose money through your investments), then the chances are that there is a problem with the #9 or #1 Facing Star. For example, one of these stars may be located in a cluttered room or in a storeroom full of junk you've hoarded for the last ten years. Or perhaps one of them is located in a palace that is missing from your property.

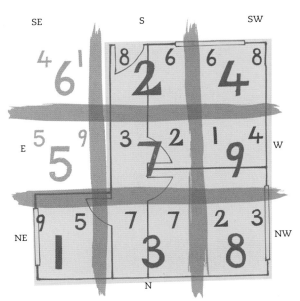

In this S2/3-facing home, the #9 and #1 Facing Stars are located in a missing area, which indicates bad luck with investments.

Let's assume you are new to investing and, having a bit of surplus cash, are looking to use classical feng shui to help you find a good place to park your surplus cash, so that your money works for you and grows. The key here is to find either the #9 or #1 Facing Star and then activate it, either by placing an aquarium or water feature in the room or by using that room as a workroom or study. The latter option is particularly beneficial if you run your own business or you rely on intellectual property to generate income (for example, if you are a writer or artist). The star will not only help you with your work but will give you opportunities to benefit financially from your ideas or intellectual property.

Don't be greedy and try to activate both stars! Pick the one that is located in a room where it's easy for you to place an aquarium or water feature or to locate your study or workroom. Keep the area spacious and airy, and the water in the aquarium clean.

This office has the #1 Facing Star. Working in this room activates this star, which is particularly good for writers, bringing financial gain.

What if you have investments but they either are not performing or, worse, have sunk in value so that you're in the red? In such instances, the problem is generally caused by the #9 or #1 Facing Star (or both) being located in a cluttered or congested area, or being missing entirely from the property.

If the problem is a cluttered or congested area, solving the problem is a matter of simply clearing out that space, de-cluttering, and airing out the room.

If you have a missing #9 or #1 Facing Star, focus on what you can use. If the #9 is missing, look for the #1; if the #1 is missing, look for the #9. Activate whichever star is present, either by placing Water in the palace where it is located, or by using more often the room where the star is located.

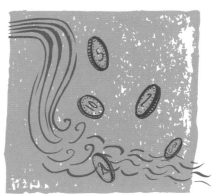

When important Wealth Stars are missing from the home, the flow of money can be badly affected.

What if both of these Facing Stars are missing?

Although it is rare for *both* the #9 and #1 Facing Stars to be absent in a property, it is possible if your property has more than one missing palace. In such a case, the ability to tap into them depends on whether the missing palaces are within the boundary of your property. If, for example, either the #9 or #1 Facing Star is located in a missing palace that is within the boundaries of your home but is not part of the building or of the living space, you can still activate the stars by placing Water in that area.

If the missing palace is not within the boundaries of your home (it may be part of a public corridor) or is simply non-existent (in the case of a courtyard or open space, for example), then you must be realistic about the situation. In these instances, you will need to focus on extremely long-term investments (ten to twenty years) and go for the most conservative means of growing your wealth. You will not be able to capitalize on opportunities that come from speculative investments.

Handling the #3 and #5 Stars

- I have a serious credit card debt—I can't keep up with repayments (it's the story of my life).

- I have serious debts (credit card, mortgage, car repayment, student loan) despite having a good job. The debt just keeps piling up.

- I have a good job which pays me a good income, but I don't know where the money goes and can't seem to save much.

This solution is suitable if you are in one of the above situations, any of which can be classified as a wealth problem revolving around a chronic inability to save money. In such instances, you may find that no matter how hard you work, there's barely enough to make ends meet. Or despite working for several years, you don't seem to have much to your name, in terms of cash or other assets. Or you simply have too much debt despite working hard and trying very hard to save.

The #5 and #3 Stars can cause loss of wealth—so check where they occur in your home's natal chart.

The typical culprit behind problems relating to an inability to save, or an inability to earn enough to make ends meet, is the #3 Facing Star or the #5 Facing Star—or in serious situations, the two stars in tandem, in a #3–#5 combination.

The primary difference between these two stars is the means by which they cause loss of wealth. With the #3 Facing Star, loss of wealth is typically caused by situations that involve fear or intimidation, such as selling investments out of panic or irrational fear, or being burgled or mugged. It can also mean loss of wealth as the result of arguments, disputes, or legal problems.

The #5 Facing Star tends to cause loss of wealth through catastrophe or disaster, such as an unexpected accident that causes injury, resulting in medical bills or an inability to work. Triggering the #5 can bring about an abrupt change in circumstances or relationships (such as a business partnership suddenly going bad) that results in a loss of money or squabbles over money. The #5 Facing Star can also bring about loss of wealth through being defrauded, embezzled, or cheated or through gambling or pyramid schemes.

To know exactly how the loss of wealth occurs, we usually need to look at the combination: which Sitting Star appears with the #3 or #5 Facing Star. That, however, is an advanced subject and so I will not delve into it too much here. The point is to appreciate that the #3 and #5 Facing Stars are the prime causes of loss of wealth, and you want to avoid having these stars in important rooms or the main door area.

Also, the #5 Facing Star is considered worse than the #3 because its effects tend to be calamitous in nature and catastrophic in outcome. So if you find yourself between the devil and the deep blue sea, the #5 is the one you really don't want to have in an important room or at the main door.

Identifying the cause of the problem

To see if you have a problem caused by the #3 or #5 Facing Star, take a look at the floor plan that has the flying stars chart of your property superimposed on it (see page 56–60). Look for the #3 and #5 Facing Stars, circle them in red, and then check whether either of these stars is located in one of the following places:

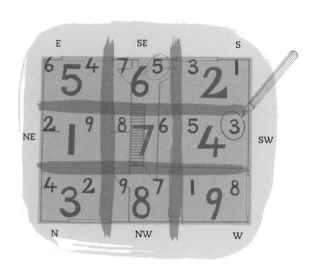

- At the main door to your home.
- In your bedroom.
- In your study, workroom, or home office.

Circle the #5 and #3 Facing Stars to identify the source of money problems. In this period 7, SE 2-facing property, the #5 Facing Star is located by the front door. To cure its negative effects, place metal objects near the door.

If the #3 or #5 is located in any of these locations, your financial challenges are doubtlessly caused by its being activated. If you find you have the #3 and #5 in the same palace (for example, the #3 Facing Star appears with the #5 Sitting Star, or vice versa), then you have a double problem! However, the situation is not impossible to address, if you are willing to make some modest changes.

In the example shown above left, the #3 and #5 Stars are located in the southwest and southeast palaces respectively. Remember, avoid using any rooms located in either of the palaces containing these stars as bedrooms or home offices, and if possible avoid using a main door that is located in either of them.

Offensive and defensive tactics

In classical feng shui, using a cure can be regarded as a defensive tactic. In other words, you're not attempting to make progress—you're just trying to prevent things from getting worse. Elemental cures are not ineffective, but they are considered in classical feng shui to be a secondary approach. Generally, we prefer to use offensive tactics instead where possible. We try to "dodge" the problem by not using that main door, say, or by staying out of a particular room—this is an example of the nuanced and subtle application of feng shui.

However, if an offensive tactic cannot be used, then an elemental cure (see pages 60–1) is better than doing nothing to counter the negative energies of a problematic star. It involves using objects made from the element that weakens the element of the star in the five-element cycle (see pages 28–9). Don't worry about whether or not the items you use have auspicious-sounding names or the right symbolic meaning. In the elemental cures of classical feng shui, what counts is what the item is made of.

Let's take a look at the possible scenarios involving the #3 and #5 Facing Stars and consider how you can resolve them.

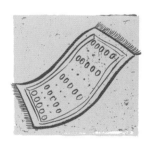

#3 or #5 Facing Star at the main door

The best offensive tactic in this situation is to find another door you can use to enter the property. This is primarily applicable to a house on its own plot of land rather than an apartment, since most houses have a back door or a side door. As far as possible, avoid using the door where the #3 or #5 Facing Star is located. If you live in an apartment, or perhaps a linked house where there is only one door to enter the property, then you have no choice and will need to utilize an elemental cure.

A red mat or rug, or an aromatherapy burner, will help cure the bad effects of the #3 Facing Star.

Elemental cure for #3 Facing Star: If you have a #3 Facing Star at the main door and you can't use another door, then place a red floor mat or carpet at your door, either inside or outside. If this is not possible, instead place an aromatherapy burner or oil lamp on a small table beside the main door, provided it is not a safety or fire hazard—it has to be kept burning. If you cannot use an oil lamp or aromatherapy burner either, then place a lamp with a red shade on a table next to the main door.

Using the metal element as a cure doesn't have to mean lots of old brass and pewter—modern metal shelving will work, too.

This cure works by weakening the #3 Star, which is of the Wood element. Red floor mats or carpets, red lampshades, and oil lamps or aromatherapy burners are all Fire items. As Fire burns Wood, it weakens Wood.

Elemental cure for #5 Facing Star: If you have a #5 Facing Star at the main door and you can't use another door, then place a small table beside the main door, or in a convenient location in the foyer just inside the main door area, and display on it large metal items, such as a lamp with a brass base, a silver vase or urn, or a bronze sculpture. The key is to make sure that you have sizable items made of metal on the table. This cure works by weakening the #5 Star, which is of the Earth element. Metal objects weaken Earth in the five-element cycle, therefore placing these Metal objects at the main door area will help to reduce some of the negative effects of the #5 Star.

#3 or #5 Facing Star in the bedroom

Here, too, the solution is to use an offensive tactic if you can. That means, essentially, moving out of the room into another room. This should always be your first course of action whenever you are confronted with a negative star in a room you are using. Of course, it is not always possible, especially if you are living in a very small space, such as a one-bedroom house or apartment or a studio apartment. In that case, you'll need to use the defensive tactic of an elemental cure.

Elemental cure for #3 Facing Star: If the #3 Facing Star is in your bedroom, replace the carpet in your room with red carpeting. You can also try having a red lampshade in your room, although this is only beneficial if you keep it on all the time—the carpet is probably a more practical option. It is not advisable to use aromatherapy lamps or oil lamps in the bedroom, because they would be a fire hazard. The red carpet and red lampshade are Fire items, and the element Fire burns Wood, which is the element of the #3 Star. By using an element that consumes Wood, we are seeking to weaken the Star's energies.

Elemental cure for #5 Facing Star: If the #5 Facing Star is in your bedroom, collect together as many Metal objects as you can, and place them in a convenient corner of your bedroom, such as on top of a chest of drawers or bedside table. Metal objects might include war medals, brass candlesticks, a silver-backed hairbrush and hand mirror set, or other items made from metal. As the #5 Star is of the Earth element, Metal is used to weaken the energies of this Star, since Earth produces Metal in the five-element cycle. It is important to use real metal objects (as opposed to objects painted in metallic paint), and the bigger they are, the better.

Metal objects such as silver picture frames are a cure for the #5 facing star in the bedroom.

#3 or #5 Facing Star in the workroom or home office

If you are self-employed or an entrepreneur, the location of the #3 or #5 Facing Star in your home office will be the reason you're having not just problems saving money, but probably difficulty making money as well. As with the previous two scenarios, the preferred course of action is to move, particularly because you are not only using a room where negative stars are located, but also using it for activities relating to your capacity to generate wealth. Ideally, you would move into a room with the #8 Facing Star (see page 85).

If you can't move your office out of the room, try at least to use it less. For example, limit your use of the room to paperwork, and avoid making important phone calls or doing work in this room. If you absolutely have no choice but to use this room for work, then install the elemental cures.

Elemental cure for #3 Facing Star: To tackle the #3 Star, you have a few options. Use a red carpet, large red rug, or red flooring in the room. If you can't do this, then put a red floor mat or small rug at the door to the room. You can also include a lamp with a red lampshade or use an aromatherapy burner or oil burner, but they have to be kept on for the duration of the time you are working. These are all Fire items, and the element Fire burns Wood, the element of the #3 Star.

To cure the #5 Facing Star, use the metal element, from trophies or medals to figurines.

Elemental cure for #5 Facing Star: To tackle the #5 Star, you could install a shelf at least three feet (one meter) long in the room and fill it with sports trophies, brass boxes, or any sizable metal objects. Either arrange them in an aesthetically pleasing manner or just line them up—the focus is on the metal objects, not how they are arranged. In the five-element cycle, Metal weakens Earth, the element of the #5 Star.

Check the #8 Star to cover your bases

Sometimes financial problems are caused by two separate yet connected situations—for example, if you work, sleep, or have the main door at either the #3 or #5 Facing Star, and your #8 Facing Star is located in a cluttered room, a storeroom, or a room that is airless and isn't used much.

In that instance, you may have to make a decision on what to do. Do you fix the #8 Star or do you solve the #3 or #5 Star problem? My advice is to focus first on what you can do easily. A problematic main door is usually the hardest problem to tackle, especially if you live in an apartment, whereas placing an aquarium or a water feature in a certain room, or using a room more/less, is generally not too difficult.

The golden rule is that something is better than nothing; action is better than inaction. Fixating on what you cannot improve is really a waste of time—focus instead on what you *can* do and how you can be proactive in solving the problem.

Resolving short-term and temporary wealth problems using the annual flying stars

Some financial situations are short-term in nature. A shortage of cash, for example, is a classic illustration of this. Think of those times in previous months when you got overzealous with your credit card and had to tighten your belt the following month. Or those months where half your friends had birthdays around the same time and you overspent on dinners or gifts, resulting in, again, belt-tightening. Or maybe you needed a little extra financial boost to enable you to buy something you wanted, like a piece of furniture or a TV. In these instances, you can identify the nature of your short-term problem and then just implement the relevant solution.

Again, it is important to be honest with yourself about the exact nature of the problem. Using a short-term solution is not the answer if you have been in the red for the last few years! Similarly, if your current credit card debt is the result of excessive retail therapy for the last year, rather than last month's clearance sale, then you should be looking at a more long-term solution (see page 82).

Using the annual flying stars for a short-term shortage of wealth problem

● *I have short-term credit card debts—I overspent last month.*

● *I have recent credit card debt or a recent debt problem—I've never had this problem before.*

● *I have always been able to save money, but lately it seems that expenses have gone up and I just don't know where my money goes.*

For any of the above situations, the annual flying stars can be deployed, as the money problem is relatively recent (within the last three to six months) and represents a big change. It is therefore an annual flying stars problem, rather than a problem in the natal flying stars chart.

Annual flying stars reference table

2008, 2017, 2026

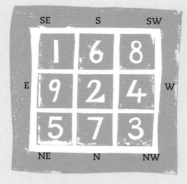

2007, 2016, 2025

2006, 2015, 2024

2005, 2014, 2023

2004, 2013, 2022

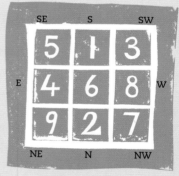

2003, 2012, 2021

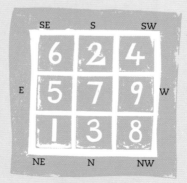

2002, 2011, 2020

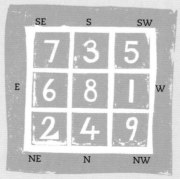

2001, 2010, 2019

2000, 2009, 2018

Step by step

Superimposing the annual flying stars chart on the floor plan

1 You first need to superimpose the annual flying stars chart onto your floor plan. Start by finding the appropriate annual flying stars chart for the present year shown in the annual flying stars reference table opposite.

2 On a fresh copy of your floor plan marked with the nine palaces, mark out the location of the nine flying stars. For example, in 2009 the #3 Star is located in the northeast palace, so you would put the numeral 3 in the northeast palace. You now have the annual flying stars chart superimposed on your floor plan.

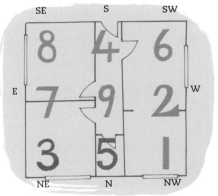

The annual flying stars chart covering the years 2000, 2009, and 2018 imposed over a floor plan.

Check the position of the annual #3 and #5 Stars

These two stars are the main culprits when it comes to problems with wealth. Look at the floor plan on which you have marked out the annual flying stars.

- Is the annual #3 or #5 Star in the palace where your main door is located?
- Is the annual #3 or #5 Star in the palace where your bedroom is located?
- Is the annual #3 or #5 Star in the palace where your workroom, home office, or study is located?

If your answer to any of the questions listed above is yes, then the annual star is what's wreaking havoc with your bank account and piling up all those expenses.

The solution to the problem depends on where the #3 or the #5 is located and upon your property itself. Overleaf, you will find the solution you can implement, depending on your situation.

Location of #3 Star
Solution

#3 is at the main door.

If you can, use another entrance to come into your home (preferably one where the annual #8, #9, or #1 Star is located).

#3 is at the main door and you cannot use another entrance.

Place a red rug or mat at the main door, or put an aromatherapy burner or an oil lamp on a table in the foyer—keep it burning at all times if it is not a fire or safety hazard. If safety is an issue, then use a lamp with a red lampshade instead.

#3 is in the bedroom.

If you can, use another room as your bedroom for the year (preferably a room where the annual #9 or #1 Star is located).

#3 is in the bedroom and you cannot use another bedroom.

Place a large red carpet in the room or a small red rug or mat at the entrance to the bedroom. You can also consider using a lamp with a red lampshade, but this has to be kept on and might not be practical. For safety reasons, aromatherapy burners and oil lamps cannot be used in bedrooms.

#3 is in the workroom, home office, or study.

If you can, use another room as your workroom, home office, or study for the year (preferably a room where the annual #8, #9, or #1 Star is located).

#3 is in the workroom, home office, or study and you cannot use another room.

Use a large red carpet or red flooring in the room, or place a small red rug or mat at the entrance to the room. You can also consider using a lamp with a red lampshade, or an aromatherapy burner or oil lamp to weaken the energies of the #3 Star. However, it has to be kept burning or at least kept on for as much of the time as possible, and especially when you are working in the room.

Location of #5 Star
Solution

#5 is at the main door.

If you can, use another entrance to come into your home (preferably an entrance where the annual #8, #9, or #1 Star is located).

#5 is at the main door and you cannot use another entrance.

Place a small table or a shelf beside the main door, and display metal items such as a silver vase or an urn, a lamp with a brass base, or a bronze sculpture here to weaken the effects of the #5 Star.

#5 is in the bedroom.

If you are able, use another room as your bedroom for the year (preferably a room where the annual #9 or #1 Star is located).

#5 is in the bedroom and you cannot use another bedroom.

Fill the top of a chest of drawers or bedside table with sizable metal items such as medals, brass candlesticks, or a silver-backed hairbrush and hand mirror set, to weaken the effects of the #5 Star.

#5 is in the workroom, home office, or study.

If you can, use another room as your workroom, home office, or study for the year (preferably a room where the annual #8, #9, or #1 Star is located).

#5 is in the workroom, home office, or study and you cannot use another room.

Fill a shelf with sizable metal items such as sports trophies or brass boxes to weaken the effects of the #5 Star. You can also place this shelf next to the entrance to the room. If you cannot put up a shelf for these items, place a good-size metal item (such as a large silver dish) on your worktable.

Using the annual flying stars for a short-term increase in wealth opportunities

● *My finances are sound but I would like to make a little extra in the next few months to afford a one-off purchase.*

● *I've just spent quite a lot on a vacation or expensive purchase and want to be able to recoup some of that money.*

For either of the above two situations, the annual flying stars can be deployed. In these two scenarios, you're looking at short-term wealth opportunities coming your way, such as some part-time work or a big contract that lands you a nice commission. Or perhaps your experiences during a recent vacation have enabled you to generate income by writing about them for a magazine. In these situations, you will want to tap into the annual #9 Star to get a little financial boost.

To use the annual #9 Star, you first need to superimpose the annual flying stars chart on your home's floor plan (see page 99), and then find the #9 star.

- Is the annual #9 Star in the palace where your main door is located?
- Is the annual #9 Star in the palace where your bedroom is located?
- Is the annual #9 Star in the palace where your workroom, home office, or study is located?

If you have answered yes to any of those questions, there's no real need for you to do anything. Just keep using these areas and the benefits of the qi of the #9 Star will soon come your way.

If your answer to any of the preceding questions was no, then you simply need to be more proactive. Are any of the following options available to you?

- I have an entrance (side door, back door) in the palace where the annual #9 Star is located.
- I have a room that I can use as a bedroom in the palace where the annual #9 Star is located.

- I have a room that I can use as a workroom, home office, study, or television room in the palace where the annual #9 Star is located.
- I can place a water feature in the annual #9 Star location.

If you answered yes to any of the above options, then you need to take action accordingly. Start using that entrance more. Move into that room with the annual #9 Star, use it for work or for poker nights, or place an aquarium in it. The important thing is to tap into the favorable qi of the annual #9 Star by using the room a lot or keeping the qi active there.

Annual stars come with expiration dates

Because qi has a dynamic, changing quality about it, annual stars come with expiration dates. This year's stars will shift positions and move to different palaces next year, and the year after. So when using the annual stars, remember that your goal must always be a short-term one (something you want to achieve within the next six to twelve months) and that to tap into the annual stars, you have to keep updating your feng shui.

The annual flying stars chart for the year 2010 imposed over a floor plan. Water features can activate the annual #9 star.

Obviously, changing rooms every single year makes absolutely no sense and there is a finite number of rooms in the house that you can use. There will be some years when the #9 Star is in your bathroom, and there's not a great deal you can do about that!

It all comes back to the long-term versus short-term approach. Remember, for consistent results and for growth in terms of your finances and bank account, always look at the natal flying stars chart of your home. For a quick fix or a little boost, use the annual flying stars chart.

As long as you remember that quick fixes are exactly that, and you keep in mind that ultimately the long-term outlook is always more important, there is no reason why classical feng shui can't help you achieve your financial goals in life.

The bottom line on feng shui and wealth

At the start of this chapter, I stated that every home has wealth qi that can be activated. The operative words here are "can be." In other words, every home has potential wealth qi in it, and whether or not it is working for you depends upon your willingness to be proactive and utilize this positive energy.

This is a no-holds-barred, school-of-hard-knocks approach to feng shui. Perhaps you feel that what you are being asked to do here is a trifle challenging. You may feel that classical feng shui is really difficult, what with all this swapping rooms, shifting places, being in a different bedroom, entering through side doors. Suddenly, putting your faith in a gold-plated resin dragon may seem rather alluring, by comparison.

But in my experience, the greatest challenge in helping people to get the best out of the qi in their home is their mindset. Human beings are often set in their ways—we dislike inconvenience, and change is, frankly, quite inconvenient. Even something as simple as changing the room we sleep in, or entering our homes through an alternative entrance, can feel

Redefining success

Your personal destiny, also known as BaZi or the Four Pillars of Wisdom (see page 41), is an important aspect of your financial situation. And because your destiny dictates the extent to which you can achieve wealth and financial success, feng shui can only help you achieve your potential to the maximum of what is defined by your destiny. It is the upper limits of what you can achieve in this life, including the measure of financial success. In effect, each of us has a cosmic glass ceiling.

That doesn't mean you have to throw in the towel, though. It just means that you may have to alter your financial ambitions. Maybe you need to have more realistic expectations about the monetary success you will achieve.

Most importantly, you may want to consider your definition of success. Do you feel that loathing your job is a necessary evil for earning as much as you need? Or is loving what you do while being moderately well-paid more important to you? Do you want your life to be measured by dollars and cents or by a sense of achievement, fulfillment, and personal happiness?

If your destiny code holds the final card, then feng shui is about how you play the game. And by using feng shui, you will know that, although you may not arrive at your destination a multimillionaire, the journey—the experiences garnered, the friends you made, the people you met—were absolutely worth the price of admission!

inconvenient or difficult because it's different. It feels weird.

In such instances, my answer is simple: just keep your eye on the prize, or goal—think of the carrot, not the stick.

You have purchased this book because you want to make a difference to your life. And you are reading this section because you want to *change* something in your life, such as your financial status or your bank balance.

Bite the bullet and change bedrooms or use another door if it is called for. Once you start seeing the benefits of tapping into the wealth qi of your home, you'll overcome your reservations about entering

through different doors, sleeping in a different room, or using a different area of the house for work.

Let's be honest: How many of us would consider that installing a simple aquarium (the absolute bare minimum you can do to activate your home's wealth qi) is a great inconvenience and an absolute waste of time? And how many of us would pass up the opportunity to gain a little monetary advantage, in exchange for a very minor inconvenience?

Every home has wealth qi that can be activated. So go forth and activate. Make that wealth qi work for you. You'll soon see that it was worth the modest effort.

Bright, clean, and spacious rooms that are used frequently can be enough to activate positive Wealth Stars in a home. Mirrors may look good, but they don't create good feng shui alone.

Chapter 4
Mentor Schmentor— Using Classical Feng Shui with Career Matters

Is it you, or is it your job? Feng shui can help determine which careers you will excel in, and which you'll find tough-going. Even when you are in the right industry and doing a job that is tailor-made for you, problems and challenges can still arise. If you're looking to rediscover your passion for your job, improve your promotion prospects, or just get along a little better with your boss, here are some effective feng shui ways to smooth the path to your ideal job.

Career problems and missing palaces

A difficulty in excelling in a particular job or industry can always be traced to a lack of connection with that industry, on an elemental level.This is primarily determined using BaZi (see page 41). However, sometimes it can also be a problem with the house.

One of the most common causes of a sluggish or lackluster career in a particular industry is the problem of a missing palace (or missing palaces—it's possible to have two missing) in the home (see pages 56 and 59). The missing palace will tell you which industry, or which type of job, you *cannot* do as long as you live in that property. Bear in mind that the industry might also be inherently ill-suited to you based on your BaZi. This would also explain why you chose to live in a house with that particular missing palace—it all makes sense in the end!

If your home does not have a missing palace, then your career problems or challenges are likely to be caused by something else. In that case, you will need to carefully evaluate the precise nature of your career problem. See pages 118–19 for more about tackling this.

Is your home undermining you?

But first, you need to rule out the possibility that the home you're in is the source of your career difficulties. The table overleaf outlines the types of industries and jobs that are represented by each of the eight directions and their Gua.

If the palace that is missing in your home is a palace that also relates to an aspect of your job, then this is an indication that perhaps you are in the wrong industry or are doing a job that is not suited to you.

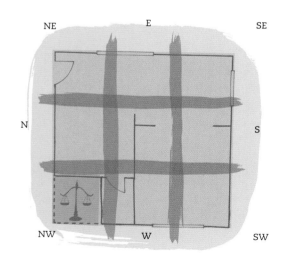

Anthony's home has a missing northwest palace, which is linked with his profession, the law. His home cannot support his career.

Example: Anthony is a lawyer but doesn't seem to be able to make much headway in his job, getting mediocre clients and work that is not of interest to him. His floor plan (shown above left) shows a missing palace. When we place the nine palaces grid over the floor plan, it is clear that the missing palace is the northwest palace. Among other things, the northwest palace relates to the judicial profession, to which Anthony belongs. It is therefore clear that his home is not supporting his endeavors at work, owing to a missing palace.

Is more than one palace involved?

In today's world, most jobs have a mixed profile—in other words, they often involve more than one palace.

Example: Louise has a job in public relations, and her job involves marketing "chick lit" books and promoting their authors. The south palace relates to public relations, but the north palace also plays a part in her job. It could also be said that the southeast palace is relevant to her job, as it involves publishing and authors.

Accordingly, it's important that you clearly define your job and the industry that you're in before you check to see if the problem is caused by a missing palace. If one of the palaces that relates to your job or industry is missing, then your career in that area will be stagnant or lackluster.

Dealing with the missing palace problem

There are two approaches to the problem of a missing palace—using offensive tactics or using defensive tactics (see page 93). The offensive approach is to rectify the missing sector. In a house surrounded by land, the most obvious way to solve the problem is through building an addition (extension) to the house in the area that is missing. Once that area becomes part of the living space of the property, the missing palace problem is solved.

Enhancing an area with the element of its missing palace

However, an addition is not always a viable solution—the area missing from your home may fall outside your property boundary, or building the addition may be too expensive. In such cases, you must resort to the defensive tactic of an elemental enhancement: enhancing the area where the missing palace is by adding more of the appropriate element.

Careers associated with the eight directions

West (Dui)

Industry: Singing, speaking, or surgery

Types of jobs: Dentist, food and beverage manager, surgeon, locksmith, watchmaker, jeweler, diamond cutter, hairstylist, insurance agent, television host or personality, master of ceremonies, sculptor, singer, craftsperson, someone who works with fine tools

Characteristics of job: Involves speech, talking, or the mouth area, or involves expression or expressive skills or craftsmanship, particularly with hands or with speech

Southwest (Kun)

Industry: Holistic and natural foods, healing and therapy, caregiving, nurturing, groups or collections of individuals (like political parties or charities), farming, animal husbandry, agriculture

Types of jobs: Health and organic food business, property business, masseur/masseuse, natural and alternative therapist, nanny, teacher, caregiver, geriatric nurse, pediatrician, nurse, farmer, horticulturist, gardener

Characteristics of job: Involves nurturing, mothering, and caring

Southeast (Xun)

Industry: Scholastic, educational, and intellectual activities, research and development

Types of jobs: University professor, teacher, educator, yoga instructor, lab technician, general technician, journalist, writer, choreographer, director

Characteristics of job: Highly intellectual, learned, related to education or learning, involves analysis, thinking, artistic or poetic skills

East (Zhen)

Industry: Active lifestyle, sports, working with items made from wood, quick movement, involves using physical strength and energy

Types of jobs: Sportsman, construction worker, timber worker, furniture maker, gym instructor, fitness instructor, personal trainer, mountain climber, stuntman, go-kart driver, Formula One racer, part of a SWAT team, military, acrobat, circus performer, martial arts practitioner

Characteristics of job: Requires physical aggression or physical speed; involves physical activity, lifting and carrying

Northeast (Gen)

Industry: Health, ceramics, children's education and welfare, hilltop resorts, meditation retreats or health spas

Types of jobs: Administration, general management, blue collar workers, government/civil servants, general manager, beauty therapist, chiropractor, osteopath, accountant, sports doctor

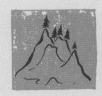

Characteristics of job: Involves healing, administration; quiet, lonely, solitary work; is related to bones

North (Kan)

Industry: Coffee bars, bars, trading, boating, yachting, transportation, tourism and hospitality, fisheries, aquatics, marine science, gifts and premiums, marketing, fast-moving consumer goods (FMCG)

Types of jobs: Marine biologist, fisherman, sailor, diver, tour guide, barman, marketing executive, spa owner, spa technician, concierge, bus driver, marketing executive

Characteristics of job: Requires mobility, flexibility, ideas, ability to perceive trends

Northwest (Qian)

Industries: Finance, law, military, banking, money markets, engineer, manufacturing, insurance, legal and judicial

Types of jobs: CEO and COO, managing director, general, judge

Characteristics of job: Requires leadership and fairness; involves money and finances

South (Li)

Industry: Food (particularly seafood) and beverage, beauty, media and public relations, oil and gas, technology, energy and heat, news or wire services, metaphysics, religion and aviation

Types of jobs: Ophthalmologist, optician, beauty salon owner, beautician, photographer, chemist, director, makeup artist, cardiologist, astronaut, feng shui practitioner, astrologer

Characteristics of job: Revolves around beauty or activities in the public eye, involves the media, relates to the heart or eyes, is high-tech in nature, or involves enlightened or metaphysical teachings

Every palace is associated with one of the five elements, and an elemental enhancement involves introducing into the area one or more objects (usually fairly large, immovable ones) made from that element.

Elemental enhancements to grow an element

Sometimes, however, it is not possible to introduce that particular element safely or practically. In that case, an elemental enhancement can involve using the element that *grows* the element of the palace. The elemental enhancement grows the element according to the five elements productive cycle (see page 29). So, for example, if you want to use a Fire elemental enhancement but can't do this safely, you can use a Wood elemental enhancement instead, as Wood grows Fire in the cycle.

Mental over elemental?

You might be wondering—what is the difference between an elemental cure and an elemental enhancement? An elemental cure is used when a needed element is missing or when we want to neutralize or weaken an unfavorable element. An elemental enhancement is used when the element is already present but just needs to be perked up and strengthened.

What to expect from elemental enhancement

Elemental enhancement is a very safe, simple, and low-cost method for getting a small career boost. However, it will not solve all your career problems. It will not mean that your career will instantly take off overnight, or that the CEO will suddenly recognize your potential when they had scarcely noticed you before, or that from a fledgling position you'll suddenly be promoted to head of the department.

However, you should be able to see a modest improvement to your career situation when you strengthen the missing palace's elements. You can expect to meet fewer obstacles in your job, and possibly be given the opportunity to shift to a position that better suits your talents and skills, or even a better job.

You should also find you have a greater sense of job satisfaction and you connect better—not just with the people at work but with the job itself. The job should become more rewarding (both in terms of the work you do and from a financial standpoint). Most importantly, you won't be given a hard time by clients or by your superior. See the table on pages 114–15 for elemental enhancements to deal with the problem of missing palaces.

To strengthen a missing palace's Metal element, you could display metal items or choose a metal chair.

Elemental enhancements for areas with missing palaces

The following table tells you which of the five elements you can use for elemental enhancement, in whichever palace(s) you are missing. As a general rule, you should pick one element that helps that sector and use that element only. Don't try to use both the elements at the same time.

For example, if you want to enhance the northwest sector, use either Metal or Earth, not the two together. You would not get double the effects by using both elements, and the resulting clutter from using both would block the qi—we want to keep things simple.

The examples have been suggested because they are relatively simple to procure and will not look bad. However, you may use any items you like, so long as they are made from the appropriate element. Being typically Chinese, Asian, or auspicious is not a prerequisite—the element the objects are predominantly made from is what matters. They should also preferably be non-movable and sizable. And as these missing-palace areas are, by definition, outside your home, they need to be weatherproof if out in the open.

Direction	Elemental enhancement associated with palace	Elemental enhancement that grows palace element
West (Dui)	METAL OBJECTS: A big metal watering can, a weatherproof bronze sculpture, or a group of large metal urns would be very appropriate.	EARTH OBJECTS: A stone birdbath, a large ceramic urn or a medium to large stone or ceramic statue will be suitable. There is no need for a specific type of statue—use whatever one you like, as long as it is sizable item, and is made of stone or ceramic. You could also construct a rock garden in this palace if space permits.
Southwest (Kun) 	EARTH OBJECTS: A large clay pot or stone urn would be useful, or you may want to place an earthenware statue or stone sculpture in this area. Make sure it is fairly sizable. Or you could fill a shelf with ceramic pots.	FIRE OBJECTS: Place an oil lamp or a lantern in this area, keeping it on all the time. An aromatherapy lamp or burner is also fine but you have to keep it burning. Use these Fire enhancements only if they are not safety hazards.
South (Li) 	FIRE OBJECTS: If possible, place a red light here, keeping it on all the time. Or use a lantern or an oil lamp and keep it burning, providing it is not a safety hazard.	WOOD OBJECTS: If you have space, you could construct a small garden or put up a shelf with lots of potted plants or hanging plants. If it is an open piece of ground, plant some beautiful flowers. If you have enough space, try to place larger, leafy plants in the area. Just make sure that the plants are not so large or so clumped together that they block out the sunlight or cause the area to become dank and congested.

Direction	Elemental enhancement associated with palace	Elemental enhancement that grows palace element
Southeast (Xun) 	WOOD OBJECTS: Potted plants, a herb garden, or a flower garden represent the element of Wood so, if space permits, you could plant a sizable flower garden here. If the space is small, fill it with as many medium-size or tall potted plants as you can. Be careful not to block out the sunlight, especially if there is a door or window. You want to make sure it stays airy and bright.	WATER OBJECTS: If the area is very small, you might be better off going with Water objects such as a fountain or other water feature. The key is to make sure the water is always clean and moving.
East (Zhen)	WOOD OBJECTS: Potted plants, a herb garden, or a flower garden represent the element of Wood, so if space permits, you can have a good-size flower garden here. If the space is small, fill it with medium-size to tall potted leafy plants.	WATER OBJECTS: If the area is very small, you might be better off going with Water objects such as a fountain or other water feature. The key is to make sure the water is always clean and moving.
Northeast (Gen) 	EARTH OBJECTS: If space permits, you can place a large stone or ceramic statue or sculpture here. For a smaller space, use a large ceramic vase or a stone birdbath. Or put up a shelf and display pottery or other ceramic items on it.	FIRE OBJECTS: If you want to use Fire, use a lantern or an oil lamp. A red light will also suffice but is less effective compared with actual burning fire. If this is a safety hazard, go for one of the Earth objects instead.
North (Kan) 	WATER OBJECTS: You can place Water here in the form of a fountain or other type of water feature, or if you have room build a small fishpond.	METAL OBJECTS: A big metal watering can, a weatherproof sculpture in bronze, or a group of large metal urns would be very appropriate.
Northwest (Qian) 	METAL OBJECTS: A big metal watering can or a group of large metal urns would be appropriate. A weatherproof bronze sculpture of generous proportions would be good, too.	EARTH OBJECTS: You could use a stone urn or bird bath, or a big clay pot. A large stone sculpture or a reasonable-size statue will work here, too. If space permits, you could even construct a modest rock garden.

You can strengthen the element of your office without resorting to wind chimes or other feng shui giveaways. Bring in the correct element in subtle ways, choosing items you like, such as chrome furniture or metallic desk lighting.

Strengthening an existing palace for a career boost

If you don't have any missing palaces in your home, can you still use elemental enhancement to give your career a little boost? Definitely! However, as the area in question is part of your living space, you have a few more options in terms of what you can utilize to enhance the palace.

It is important to make sure the qi is moving in that area. So the first thing to do is to pick the palace (or two palaces) that most closely relate to your industry and your primary job function (see pages 110–11). Now, check to see if they are cluttered rooms, or perhaps musty, airless rooms that are not used often. If that is the case, then de-clutter them and tidy them up—this will move the qi around. Also open the windows to let some air in so that the qi can circulate.

Elemental enhancements for an existing palace

Direction	Elemental enhancement associated with palace	Elemental enhancement that grows palace element
West (Dui)	METAL OBJECTS: Put up a shelf to display lots of metal items like pewterware, sports trophies, or brass or silver items.	EARTH OBJECTS: A medium to large stone sculpture will also suffice for this area.
Southwest (Kun)	EARTH OBJECTS: This is a good place for a large ceramic vase, a shelf of pottery items, or a display rack of a china collection.	FIRE OBJECTS: An oil lamp or aromatherapy burner that is kept lit is a good example of a Fire object. However, you can also construct a fireplace here (using it often during the cold months if possible) or place an electric heater here.
South (Li)	FIRE OBJECTS: An oil lamp or lit aromatherapy burner is fine but you can also construct a fireplace here, open up a skylight, or place a heater here.	WOOD OBJECTS: If this is a work or study area, you can site a large wooden bookcase for your book collection here, or include a wood carving to introduce the Wood element.
Southeast (Xun)	WOOD OBJECTS: Potted plants can be placed here to introduce the Wood element but you can also place a tall wooden cupboard or a sizable wood carving here.	WATER OBJECTS: If the area is very small, you might be better off going with Water objects, such as an aquarium or a modest water feature.
East (Zhen)	WOOD OBJECTS: Place a generous wooden cupboard or bookshelf or a large wood carving in this area.	WATER OBJECTS: If the area is very small, you could opt for Water objects—an aquarium or a modest water feature would be suitable.
Northeast (Gen)	EARTH OBJECTS: If space permits, you can place a large stone statue or sculpture here. If it is a small space, use a large ceramic vase or fill a shelf with pottery or other ceramic items, or a display rack with a china collection.	FIRE OBJECTS: This is a great place to build a fireplace or to use a heater. If you have the space and budget, you could add a skylight in the ceiling here. You can also place an oil lamp or a lit aromatherapy burner here, provided that safety is not an issue.
North (Kan)	WATER OBJECTS: You can place Water here in the form of an aquarium or a small water feature.	METAL OBJECTS: A shelf displaying brassware, silverware, or sports trophies will work here, as will a metal sculpture or a metal statue.
Northwest (Qian)	METAL OBJECTS: You could use brassware, silverware, or sports trophies on a shelf here. A metal sculpture or statue will also work well.	EARTH OBJECTS: Place a stone sculpture or statue here or a large ceramic vase.

Specific career challenges

Let's say that your career is doing fine, but you're facing a number of obstacles at work just now that are making things difficult or challenging for you. In this section, I have picked a few common career obstacles and suggested ways in which to handle these problems. These are problems that I hear about time and time again, during feng shui or BaZi consultations.

Again, it's important that you give some thought to the nature of the problem you are facing at work. If you can pinpoint an underlying problem, try to solve that first. Take a look at the checklist on the opposite page and see which scenario best describes your situation, and then turn to the solution on the pages indicated.

Problems with authority and influence

- *I am the head of my department or division, but I don't have the power and authority I need to get things done.*
  - *No one respects me at work, despite my senior position or despite my abilities.*
  - *I have a great job, but I seem to be permanently stuck at the same level or department, no matter how well I perform.*

Use the space with the #6 Sitting Star for a quiet activity such as meditation. If it falls in your office try to sit where the star is located.

If any of the above scenarios describes a problem you have at work at the moment, then you have a problem with your authority and influence. This problem, however, is quite easy to solve—you will need to look for the #6 Sitting Star in your home.

Take out the floor plan on which you have superimposed the natal flying stars chart of your home (see pages 56–60) and look for the location of the #6 Sitting Star (see the circled number on the illustration, left).

Problem	Solution
● *I am the head of my department or division, but I don't have the power and authority I need to get things done.*	See "Problems with authority and influence" (left).
● *No one respects me at work, despite my senior position or despite my abilities.*	See "Problems with authority and influence" (left).
● *I have a great job, but I seem to be permanently stuck at the same level or department, no matter how well I perform.*	See "Problems with authority and influence" (left) and also "Smoothing the climb up the greasy career pole" (page 124).
● *My boss is lazy and overworks me.*	See "Problems with your boss" (page 120).
● *My boss hates my ideas and never has anything good to say about my suggestions.*	See "Problems with your boss" (page 120).
● *I keep getting passed up for promotions, no matter how well I perform.*	See "Smoothing the climb up the greasy career pole" (page 124).

You can then do one of the following in that room in order to trigger the qi of the Sitting Star:

- Use the room for a passive activity such as sleeping or resting.
- Keep the area very still and quiet and place a yin object such as a large bookcase or shelf or a large, heavy, still object (perhaps a sizable stone statue or sculpture, or even just a large stone) in the room to support the #6 Sitting Star.

In addition, if you are able to plot the natal flying stars chart of your office or workplace, and if you are also able to dictate where your office is located, then try to sit in the palace that has the #6 Sitting Star.

In your study: #6 Sitting Star or #8 Facing Star?

One of the biggest challenges faced by newcomers to feng shui is the problem of conflicting information. It is easy to be thrown by the sheer quantity of information and also by the fact that sometimes a room may be good for one thing but not for another. These make it seem as though there is contradictory information. In reality, there is no contradiction in feng shui—more often than not, the confusion has arisen because people are trying to make a room achieve more than one aim. They want the wealth and they want the good relationships, and they want to get it all out of one room!

A good example of this seeming conundrum is the study. In Chapter 3, I indicated that one way to activate the #8 Facing Star for wealth is to use the room where the #8 Facing Star is located as a study or home office. This is because work is considered a yang activity and thus suited for the #8 Facing Star. In this chapter, I have indicated that you can use any room with a #6 Sitting Star as a study or for passive, yin activity, in order to assist you with problems of authority and influence.

That may seem inconsistent, but it's not, because a room can be used for both passive and active activities. For some of us, the study is a place of relaxation, where we read, listen to music, maybe surf the Internet, or just play computer games—it is a personal sanctuary. For others, the study is a place of work.

In Chapter 3, solutions for wealth-related problems were being considered, hence in that instance we were looking at the study as a place of work. In this chapter, however, we are looking at solutions for people- and relationship-related problems, and so the study is suggested as a place of relaxation. Remember, Facing Stars help us deal with problems related to wealth, and Sitting Stars with problems related to people and relationships.

To avoid misunderstandings, keep things simple. Use a room for just one goal (wealth or career) rather than multiple goals, and focus on using either the Facing Star or the Sitting Star. Thus, if you utilize a Sitting Star such as the #6 Sitting Star, which is triggered by yin or passive activity, then use the room as a place for relaxation. If your goal is to utilize a Facing Star, such as the #8 Facing Star, a star triggered by yang or positive activity, then use the room for work.

Problems with your boss

- *My boss is lazy and overworks me.*
- *My boss hates my ideas and never has anything good to say about my suggestions.*

If either of the above scenarios describes your situation at work, you need to find someone who will be your cheerleader, who will speak up for you or will come in and help relieve your workload. The trick here is to activate your Personal Nobleman Star. Doing this involves a slightly different approach. Instead of referring to the natal flying stars chart of your house, use the floor plan that has the 24 Mountains superimposed on it (see pages 62–3). To activate the Personal Nobleman, you simply need to identify the sector in your home where it resides (see page 123), and then place a water feature or a small aquarium there to activate the star's qi (see page 87).

This San He technique (see page 19) is invaluable because it is personalized. Each individual has a Personal Nobleman Star allocated to them, and when you utilize this star the favorable effects will accrue to you only. This is because the technique specifically uses your year of birth—in particular, the Heavenly Stem of your year of birth—to determine the location of the Personal Nobleman Star.

What is a Nobleman?

If you find you're often left in the lurch at work, with no one to help you out of a situation, or you seem to have only detractors rather than supporters at your workplace, then you have a Nobleman problem. The term essentially refers to people who are helpful to you at work and in life. They can appear in many manifestations, such as a helpful

boss, a senior worker who sees it as their job to help their junior, or maybe a CEO who sees a lot of similarities between you and themself and so gives you a leg-up from behind the scenes. It could be a sympathetic clerk at a government office, or a spouse who always manages to suggest intelligent solutions. Noblemen also include suppliers and clients who give you repeat business or recommend you to people. Of course, the Nobleman can actually be either male or female.

Having Noblemen is important in one's career. While a lack of them doesn't preclude advancement, having them is a useful little boost. To tap into this valuable informal resource, all you need to do is activate your Personal Nobleman Star.

Whatever your business, finding and activating your Personal Nobleman Star in your home encourages mentors to help you to advance your career at the office.

Of heavenly and earthly matters

Most people know that each year has an animal sign (see page 37) attached to it, but did you know that there's an elemental value attached to each of the animal signs? For example, 2008 is known as the year of the Earth Rat, while 2009 is the year of the Earth Ox.

In the Chinese calendar, each year, which is called a Pillar, is represented by a Heavenly Stem (the elemental value of the year—Water, Fire, Earth, Metal, or Wood) and an Earthly Branch (in simple terms, the animal sign of the year).

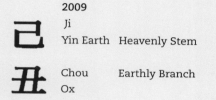

2009
己 Ji
Yin Earth   Heavenly Stem

丑 Chou   Earthly Branch
Ox

The ten Heavenly Stems, consisting of the yin and yang versions of the five elements, are shown below:

Typically, the Heavenly Stems are referred to by their technical names, but beginners usually are more comfortable using their yin and yang variant names. So, for example, yin Water is known as Gui and yang Earth is known as Wu. We usually don't add the elemental quality to the name because it's understood that Gui = yin Water. As you advance in your understanding of classical feng shui, and if you study BaZi (see page 41), you will become familiar with these names. But for now, stick to what you can remember—if calling it yin Earth sticks in your mind better, then go with that. And if you find that calling it Ji Earth is easier for you to recall, then go with that.

There are twelve Earthly Branches. Each has a greater representation within classical feng shui, and also BaZi, than its animal sign. They have their own technical names. At this point you simply need to know your own personal animal sign but it's useful to be aware that they are more than just animal signs. The twelve Earthly Branches are shown below:

Chinese character	Phonetic pronunciation	Polarity (yin/yang) and element
甲	Jia	Yang Wood
乙	Yi	Yin Wood
丙	Bing	Yang Fire
丁	Ding	Yin Fire
戊	Wu	Yang Earth
己	Ji	Yin Earth
庚	Geng	Yang Metal
辛	Xin	Yin Metal
壬	Ren	Yang Water
癸	Gui	Yin Water

Chinese character	Phonetic pronunciation	Animal sign
寅	Yin	Tiger
卯	Mao	Rabbit
辰	Chen	Dragon
巳	Si	Snake
午	Wu	Horse
未	Wei	Goat
申	Shen	Monkey
酉	You	Rooster
戌	Xu	Dog
亥	Hai	Pig
子	Zi	Rat
丑	Chou	Ox

Step by step

How to find and activate your Personal Nobleman Star

1   To find your Nobleman Star, you first need to know the Heavenly Stem of the year of your birth—refer to the Year Pillar table on page 174 to find this. (The first Chinese word is the Heavenly Stem—for example, for 2009, it is Ji.) Now refer to the table at the bottom of this page to determine where your Nobleman Star is located.

2   Look at the floor plan of your house that has the 24 Mountains demarcated (see pages 62–3). There are two possible locations for the Personal Nobleman Star, so color both areas with a highlighter.

3   In whichever area or room is more practical, activate the star by adding a small water feature, an aquarium, a container with water plants, or even just a very large jar of water. The bigger the living area, the larger it needs to be. The water must be kept clean (and, if possible, moving). For more about this, see page 134.

Example: Shawn was born in 1980. He's having some problems at work and thinks he could do with some help from his Personal Nobleman. His house faces south 1, which is the Bing direction (157.6–172.5 degrees). On page 124 is the floor plan of his house, with the 24 Mountains marked. 1980 is the year of the yang Metal Monkey, or Geng Shen. The Heavenly Stem of the year is Geng, or yang Metal. Referring to the Personal Nobleman

Year of birth Heavenly Stem	Direction where Nobleman Star resides
Jia, Wu, or Geng	Ox (northeast 1) and Goat (southwest 1)
Yi or Ji	Rat (north 2) and Monkey (southwest 3)
Bing or Ding	Pig (northwest 3) and Rooster (west 2)
Xin	Tiger (northeast 3) and Horse (south 2)
Ren or Gui	Snake (southeast 3) and Rabbit (east 2)

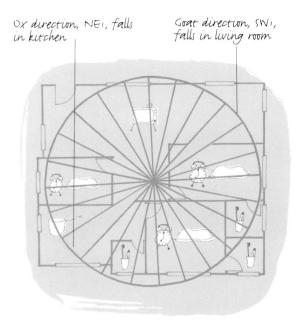

Ox direction, NE1, falls in kitchen

Goat direction, SW1, falls in living room

Star table on page 123, we know that the Personal Nobleman Star for those who have been born in a Geng year is located in the Ox (northeast 1) and Goat (southwest 1) directions. Therefore, on his floor plan, Shawn is able to highlight the two areas where the Personal Nobleman Star resides. He notes that the Ox direction spans the kitchen area of his house, while the Goat direction mainly falls within the living room area. Since the Goat sector in his house (the living room) is a more practical location for a water feature than the Ox direction (the kitchen), Shawn decides to locate it in that area to activate the Personal Nobleman Star.

Shawn was born in 1980, so his Personal Nobleman Star is located in the Ox and Goat directions, which in his south 1-facing house relate to areas of the kitchen and living room.

Smoothing the climb up the greasy career pole

- *I have a great job, but I seem to be permanently stuck at the same level or department, no matter how well I perform.*
- *I keep getting passed up for promotions, no matter how well I perform.*

If either of the above scenarios describes your work problem, you could do with some help in the promotion stakes. You may have noticed that the first scenario—being "permanently stuck at the same level or department"—has already been dealt with on page 118, under "Problems with Authority and Influence." In my view, it isn't unusual for life's problems to have more than one cause, and we find this is often the case when implementing feng shui.

As a consultant practitioner, I find that having a good understanding of how the working world and corporate world function is integral to achieving success with feng shui. For most people, being stuck at the same level at work only rankles when they lack not only power and influence but also a position. It is rare for someone to be unhappy with their position despite having tremendous power and influence. I suppose we all understand intrinsically the concept of "power behind the throne"!

"Problems with Authority and Influence" deals with the problem of being stuck at the same level or department from the standpoint of enhancing your influence and power. In that context, it's not about your job title or position, but more about what you can "do" or "achieve." You have no issues with not having a grand title, a high position, or a key to the executive bathroom—you just want to have the power to, say, make decisions, approve projects, or have the boss or chairman of the board take your view over that of your superior.

By contrast, here I'm going to discuss this problem from the standpoint of getting an improvement in the job title or job position and accompanying perks. You are not necessarily interested in having more influence or power (which often comes with more responsibility!) but you want, perhaps, a better office, more leave, better perks that come with being a rung higher up on the career ladder.

If you think you deserve a promotion and an opportunity comes up for you to apply for one, then what you need is a little feng shui to improve your chances of actually landing the promotion. Here, you will use the annual flying stars rather than the natal chart. Specifically, you are looking to activate the annual #9 Star in your home.

Step by step

Activating the annual #9 Star

1   To activate the annual #9 Star, start by looking up the annual flying stars chart for the present year (see page 98). Identify the palace where the annual #9 Star resides for the year.

Activate the annual #9 Star with an aquarium only if you can't use that room as a bedroom, workroom, or study.

2   On the floor plan of your home on which you have superimposed the nine palaces, find the palace where the #9 Star resides.

3   If possible, use the room where the annual #9 Star is located as a bedroom, a workroom, or a study. If you cannot do this, then place an aquarium in that room to activate the annual #9 Star—but only if the annual #9 Star is in the SE, E, N, or SW. If it resides in the W, NW, S, or NE, use a Fire feature instead of the aquarium.

A question of authority

In classical feng shui we differentiate between power and position. You can be in a position but lack power, or you can have power but no position. Or you can be in a position of power, both having the position and wielding the power that goes with it.

It is not uncommon these days for companies to give employees what I call "name promotions." You might get a new, more impressive-sounding title, a nice office instead of your former cubicle, a few more responsibilities, and perhaps some subordinates, but your hands are still tied when it comes to decision-making. You may be nominally closer to the boss, but his assistant probably gets consulted more often than you do. This is promotion without power.

If you are looking to gain a promotion that affords you not just the perks (better pay, more impressive title, bigger office, reserved parking space) but also the power and influence, then you have to use two stars in tandem: the annual #6 and #9 Stars.

Acitivating the #6 and the #9 Stars brings power and influence.

Obviously, you cannot be in two places at one time. But the beauty of classical feng shui is that activation of a star can occur through more than one means. Where you want to use both the annual #6 and #9 Stars, the key is to use the #6 and activate the #9. How do you use one star and activate the other? You use the annual #6 by using its location as a bedroom, workroom, or study, and you activate the annual #9 by placing an aquarium or a water feature where this star is located.

Using both the annual #6 and #9 Stars in your office would obviously be more of a challenge than at home. However, if you are able to determine the location of your office or cubicle and can also add a water feature to it, then you can tap into the annual #6 and #9 at your workplace, too. Just remember to sit at the #6 and place the aquarium or water feature at the #9, not the other way around.

Prioritize, prioritize, prioritize!

It's quite possible that your career is suffering from a plethora of issues, in which case you may be uncertain as to what you should try to deal with first. It's important not to attempt to do everything and apply all at one time the techniques I have shared with you here. That would be a

The annual #9 Star at work

If you can move the location of your desk or cubicle at the office (which is often possible in companies that encourage "hot desks" or desk swapping), try to sit at the location of the annual #9 Star for optimized feng shui results when it comes to promotions.

To do this, you need to get a floor plan of your office area and divide it up using the nine palaces grid, marking out the respective directions—N, S, E, W, NE, NW, SE, SW.

Because we're just using the annual flying stars chart, you don't need to take a direction for your office building or ascertain the natal chart of the office. You

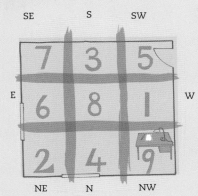

Locate the annual #9 star in your office, and sit there.

only need to know which areas of the office relate to which direction. Therefore, all you have to do is stand in the center of your office, and using your compass,

ascertain the locations of the four cardinal directions—north, south, east, and west. From there, it is easy to demarcate the rest of the palaces.

Once you have worked out the location of the nine palaces within your office, try to have your desk in the palace where the annual #9 Star is located. Then for that year you will find your path toward promotion is substantially smoothened.

If you can't do this, then use the annual #9 Star at home. Remember, some action is better than no action, and if you can't control where you sit at work, you can definitely control where you sit, work, or sleep at home.

recipe for disaster, especially for a beginner. Aim for just one goal and take just one step at a time. After you have achieved that, then move on to the next one.

Clearly, the most pressing problem should always be addressed first. For most people, having more support at work goes a long way, as it helps them feel less unable to cope with their job. If you do find that your career is beset with all kinds of challenges, activating the Personal Nobleman Star (see page 123) would probably be the best course of action. Later, as things stabilize, you could give some thought to what is next on your agenda of career to-do's.

Using classical feng shui is not difficult, but it requires a measure of proactive commitment to improving your situation. This commitment includes making it a point to understand your own problem, and then taking the right action to solve it. It could mean making a hard decision about whether a job is right for you, or perhaps consciously choosing to put more effort into your job. Think of feng shui like a pair of wings. It is not much use unless you make the leap in the first place, but once you do, then it can help you soar to new heights.

You do have to be patient—whatever changes take place will not turn you into an overnight sensation. But remember, doing something, and making an attempt to improve things, is better than doing nothing.

Office and workroom rules

If you work at home, it's important to make sure that your home office conforms to the important internal forms set out below. If you work elsewhere, you may not be able to ascertain the flying stars chart of your workplace or be able to place your office or desk in a specific location to tap into the flying stars. In that case, it is all the more important that you make sure your work area, whether it is a desk or an office, doesn't breach any of the following rules on internal forms.

Workspace do's

- Do work in a room that is bright, receives natural morning sunlight if possible, and is airy. Periodically open the windows to let the qi circulate.
- Do work in a spacious room if possible. If you are in an open-plan office, try to avoid having too many desks clustered together.
- Do have your desk facing your Personal Favorable direction, if you can. If not, just make sure you don't breach any of the Don'ts listed below.

Workspace don'ts

- Don't have your desk located directly under a beam.
- Don't sit with your back directly to the door or to a corner.
- Don't sit in a room (or locate your desk in an area) where the ceiling slants downward. If you have no choice, sit where the ceiling is the highest.
- If your office has a door, keep the area in front of the door wide and spacious; avoid having a narrow space in front of the door.

Whenever possible, work in a spacious, well-ventilated room with natural light.

Beware the bookshelves?

According to New Age feng shui, bookshelves give off sha qi and so you should not sleep or sit facing a bookshelf. Here's the logic—bookshelves look like blades, therefore when you sit opposite them you are being cut by a multitude of blades, or "poison arrows."

The logical conclusion to this is that the deadliest place in the world, the place with absolutely the worst feng shui, must be the public library. Librarians all around the world, who walk the aisles of libraries every day, with thousands of bookshelf poison arrows pointing at them, must have either the worst health or the worst professional and personal lives.

If that is the case, we must ask ourselves how on earth did Laura Bush, a librarian, manage to marry the future President of the United States and become the First Lady?

Chapter 5
Breaking your Love Duck— Relationships and Feng Shui

The classical texts of feng shui—the Green Satchel Classics, the Heavenly Jade Classics, and the Purple White Scripts—may not speak of ways in which to attain eternal love or live happily ever after, but classical feng shui can still boost your love life. It just requires an intelligent adaptation of the classical theories to handle the demands of modern life. In this chapter, you'll find lots of help with fostering harmonious relationships, enhancing your attractiveness, and improving your odds in the search for true love.

Modern practitioners of classical feng shui place personal relationships, including marriage, within the context of "people luck," also called people matters (and not to be confused with man luck—see page 9). This concept encompasses a broad range of matters, from networking to fertility. It includes health and well-being, feelings, character, behavior, friendships, and professional relationships.

In the old days, people luck essentially meant having smooth relationships with everyone in your family and in your professional life, and also having lots of children, grandchildren, and great-grandchildren. This is what led modern practitioners of classical feng shui to associate people luck with personal relationships, including your love life. Clearly, if you don't enjoy a good relationship with your wife, you are not going to have a great deal of children, and if you don't have a good relationship with your children, then, arguably, they are not going to want to be around you.

You might still have to kiss a toad, but it won't hop away!

"A little spritz of Chanel No. 5 doesn't mean the person will instantly fall head over heels in love with you, but it does make you more appealing"

Although classical feng shui doesn't offer a prescription for love, there are some specific techniques you can use to improve your chances of finding Mr or Ms Right. These techniques increase your likability, perk you up in the charm department, give you a little pizzazz in the attractiveness arena, and, of course, improve how you connect with people. They are not sweeteners or clinchers in the high-stakes game of romance, but they help.

Think of these techniques in the same way that you would regard perfume: A little spritz of Chanel No. 5 doesn't mean the person will instantly fall head over heels in love with you, but it does make you more appealing.

Being likable, being perceived as attractive (not only physically but also intellectually), and, perhaps most importantly, having the ability to relate to another person and be on the same wavelength, are crucial steps toward forming a positive and lasting relationship with a member of the opposite sex.

Equally, a strong connection and a sense of affinity with your other half are integral to the continued success of any relationship or marriage. The goal is not just finding love but also keeping it going. Thus, classical feng shui also has techniques and methods to tackle some of the problems that can complicate, jeopardize, or ruin a relationship. Think adulterous relationships, infidelity, scandalous behavior, and, of course, interfering third parties.

In matters of the heart, a lot also depends on the astrology factor. Feng shui can help, but it also has to be the right time for you to meet someone, if you want the relationship to last and succeed. If the qi is not with you, or the timing is not right, an entire houseful of mandarin ducks is not going to change things.

Classical feng shui emphasizes going with the flow of the qi, as does Chinese astrology. So if the universe is sending you a sign to say that maybe now is not the right time to seek out Prince Charming or Sleeping Beauty, taking the hint may well be the smartest thing to do.

The quackery of love ducks

Most of the New Age feng shui love trinkets are probably drawn from Chinese culture, superstition, or artistic symbolism. Mandarin ducks for example, called Yin Yiong, culturally symbolize marital bliss because the ducks swim together in pairs. If you buy into this idea, then, logically, you don't have to use ducks. A pair of any monogamous animals will do—such as lizards, emperor penguins, or vultures, since all these animals mate for life. I have no problem with symbolism, nor with the practice of psyching yourself up. One should never discount the value of positive thinking or psychological boosts. But that is not the same as blind faith in the power of an object to change things overnight. Instead of buying New Age trinkets that guarantee you a great love life, try some of the techniques in this book, such as tapping into your Personal Peach Blossom Star (see page 134) or using the Early Heaven Sitting Star combination (see page 140), to help you in your search for true love.

Feng shui can help your romantic prospects but it doesn't automatically mean instant marriage.

Your Personal Peach Blossom Star

This San He technique is good if you are single and don't have much luck on the dating scene, or if you want to meet more people. By helping you tap into the energies of your Personal Peach Blossom Star, the technique can help you improve your likability and attractiveness. But although it will open the door to romantic possibilities, it does not guarantee a successful outcome. That part comes from your own effort, meaning the 33 percent man luck contribution to the cosmic equation.

Each person has a Personal Peach Blossom Star or direction within their home. When you utilize this star, the favorable effects will benefit you and you alone in that property.

The technique uses your year of birth, specifically the Earthly Branch, as the point of reference. As explained on page 122, the earthly branch of the year of birth is what most people know as their animal sign. You will also need a floor plan of your home with the 24 Mountains demarcated (see pages 62–3). Activation of the Personal Peach Blossom Star is through the use of a vase or container with water-growing plants, placed at your Personal Peach Blossom direction.

By activating your Peach Blossom Star, you can become more attractive to other people and boost your romance prospects.

The lowdown on water features

I get many questions (and photographs) from people asking me whether the object they have purchased is a good water feature or the right water feature or a suitable water feature. They might wonder, for example, if activating the Peach Blossom Star requires a special water feature (a cupid motif water feature perhaps?).

There is no such thing as a right or wrong water feature, although sometimes we may recommend variations. Most of the time, an aquarium or any container of water will do. However, if we want to introduce the element of Wood into the equation as well (as in the case of activating the Peach Blossom Star), then we may add some plants to the mix. Most of the time, though, the term water feature just means a container with water in it.

I always try to recommend something that is practical, expedient, not unattractive, easy to maintain, and non-intrusive. Much more important is the size of the feature, which should be proportionate to the size of the residence. Obviously, an aquarium 14 inch (35 centimeter) square might do in a 400 square foot (37 square meter) studio apartment, but it certainly will not be big enough for a large home. It's also important to keep the water clean.

If you are not over-concerned about its appearance, just fill up a good-size transparent cookie jar or a modest-size plastic aquarium with water (leaving the lid off) and place it in the appropriate corner. A nice container of water plants will also do (but make sure there is plenty of water). I like to have some movement in the tank or container, so I usually suggest immersing a little pump that produces air bubbles in the tub or tank of water. Or you can have fish if you prefer, although they require a bit more maintenance. If it's not convenient to have a pump or fish, just make sure you change the water frequently in the tank or tub to keep it clean.

Kick-start your Peach Blossom luck with a water feature, appropriate to the size of your home, preferably containing growing plants or fish to keep the water active.

Finding your Personal Peach Blossom Star

Year of birth Earthly Branch	24 Mountains direction where Personal Peach Blossom Star resides
Monkey, Rat, or Dragon	Rooster (west 2 or 277.6–292.5 degrees)
Tiger, Horse, or Dog	Rabbit (east 2 or 82.6–97.5 degrees)
Pig, Rabbit, or Goat	Rat (north 2 or 352.6–7.5 degrees)
Snake, Rooster, or Ox	Horse (south 2 or 172.6–187.5 degrees)

Step by step

Activating your Personal Peach Blossom Star

1 Identify the Earthly Branch, or animal sign, of your year of birth. For example, if you were born in 1965, your Earthly Branch or animal sign is the Snake.

2 Using the table above, locate the direction where your Personal Peach Blossom Star resides. For example, if you were born in the year of the Snake, it resides in the Horse direction, or south 2.

3 Refer to the floor plan of your house, with the 24 Mountains demarcated (see pages 62–3). Locate the room or area of your house where the Peach Blossom Star resides. You may wish to highlight this area for easy reference.

4 Place a vase with clear water, a calm water feature, or a water plant in this area to activate the Peach Blossom Star.

The plant connection

When activating the Peach Blossom Stars, I have specifically asked you to use a vase with plants that grow in water rather than an ordinary aquarium or simple water feature. This isn't a random aesthetic request, but a remedy drawn from the five elements, and also based on the elemental quality of the flying stars we are looking to utilize.

Water-loving plants such as bamboo help activate Peach Blossom Stars for love luck.

The #1 Star represents Water, and the #4 Star represents Wood.

Plants in water are essentially a feature that combines Wood with Water. In the study of flying stars, this represents the #1 Star (Water) and the #4 Star (Wood). These two stars are the ones that are associated with good relationships and positive affinity, and that help foster connections between people. When a vase or container with water-growing plants is placed in a Peach Blossom Star direction, it helps activate the qi and encourages it to be more active.

As with aquariums, it is important to keep the water in the container clean. Dirty water will lead to complicated or unfavorable, negative relationships. This is because the qi becomes contaminated and impure—much like the nature of the relationship!

Here are a few key pointers for water features with plants in them:

- You can use fresh flowers but this can be expensive in the long run, so consider some hardy water-growing plants. In Asia, we usually use bamboo plants, which are hardy and cheap and which love to stand in water.
- The container should preferably be transparent, so that the water and plants can be seen fully.
- Choose a fairly large container—small vases do not usually contain enough water, even for use in a modest-size home. Be sure to change the water on a regular basis.

One of the easiest mistakes to make, which would nullify the efficacy of this technique, is to get the Earthly Branch, or animal sign, of your year of birth wrong. This would lead to the activation of the wrong Peach Blossom Star.

Classical feng shui follows the solar calendar, not the lunar calendar. Accordingly, to determine whether or not you belong to the animal sign of a certain year, make sure your birthday falls after February 4th of that year. If your birthday falls in January or within the first three days of February, you belong to the animal sign of the previous year.

Knowing your stem from your branch

To quickly refresh your memory, every year is known as a Pillar and consists of a Heavenly Stem and an Earthly Branch (see page 122). On page 123, I showed you how to find your Personal Nobleman Star using the Heavenly Stem of your year of birth as a reference point. Here, we use the Earthly Branch to find the Personal Peach Blossom Star.

An easy way to remember which is which is that the Heavenly Stem is always a yin or yang variant of one of the five elements (for example, yin Water, yang Earth) and the Earthly Branch is always one of the animal signs.

Example: Rachel was born in 1976. Her birthday is in March, so the Earthly Branch of her year of birth is the Dragon. Her home's floor plan is shown on the right, with the 24 Mountains superimposed on it. Referring to the table above, we know that the Personal Peach Blossom Star for a person born in the year of the Dragon is in the Rooster direction, or west 2 direction. From the floor plan, we can see that the Rooster direction in Rachel's house encompasses her study room. Rachel simply has to put a vase with water-growing plants in that location to activate her Personal Peach Blossom Star.

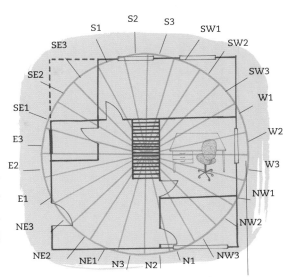

W2/3 is the Rooster direction

Can't find Mr or Ms Right?

If you have no problem attracting suitors or admirers, you probably already have Peach Blossom Stars in your BaZi chart (see page 41), but that doesn't mean you're any better off than those who have difficulty meeting someone. You might not have trouble meeting eligible people, but what if you find you keep attracting the wrong type of person?

For most people, finding someone is not like picking vegetables in the market—it's not a case of "anything will do as long as it's not rotten." We all aspire to meet someone we believe to be our soul mate, our predestined other half.

If your biggest romantic challenge is finding Mr or Ms Right, try this flying stars method to help improve the odds. The technique comes with a caveat, however: The extent of success is dependent on your astrology chart at the time when you implement the technique. If you are going through a month or perhaps a year, or "Luck Pillar," that is conducive to meeting your soul mate, this technique can expedite matters.

If you are not in a favorable luck period, then perhaps you will need to be more proactive—in other words, use the feng shui while also actively making an effort. Or maybe you ought to stop looking for Mr or Ms Right and just enjoy playing the field. You might even want to give some thought to whether you should, for now, concentrate on other aspects of your life, such as your career.

Rachel needs to place a vase or some other container of water with growing plants, such as bamboo, in her Peach Blossom sector of W2/3, which falls in her home office.

This technique, called the Early Heaven Sitting Star combination, is derived from the Early Heaven Ba Gua (see page 27). In classical feng shui this governs people matters, which encompass health issues, relationships (both personal and professional), and feelings such as contentment and happiness, which are internal or yin in nature. The technique pairs the flying star that represents *you* (so insuring there is a high degree of personalization), with a specific Sitting Star in the natal chart of your house, based on the Early Heaven Ba Gua combinations.

To use the Early Heaven Sitting Star combination, you will need:

- Your Personal Gua number (see page 174).
- The floor plan of your home with the natal flying stars chart superimposed on the plan (see pages 56–60).

Step by step

Using the Early Heaven Sitting Star combination

1 Refer to the Year Pillar & Gua Number table (see page 174) to find out your Personal Gua, based on your year of birth and your gender.

Personal Sitting	
Gua	Star
1	6
2	7
3	8
4	9
6	1
7	2
8	3
9	4

2 Using the table on the left, identify the Sitting Star that forms the Early Heaven Sitting Star combination with your Personal Gua.

3 Refer to the floor plan of your home that has the natal flying stars chart superimposed on it (see pages 56–60). Find and circle the relevant Sitting Star that combines with your Personal Gua to complete the Early Heaven Sitting Star combination.

4 Use that room or area as your bedroom, study area, meditation room, or relaxation room.

If the Sitting Star you need to use falls in a storeroom or a small area like an attic or broom closet, you obviously won't be able to use that area much. Instead, try to make sure that the qi in that room is not congested or obstructed. Tidy it up, open the door periodically to let in fresh qi, or open the windows frequently to clear out the stagnant qi.

Similarly, you can "move the qi" by periodically reorganizing, cleaning up, beautifying, or tidying up an area. Obviously this is not as good as using the area personally, but at least you know that you have minimized the obstacles to your romantic goals.

Example: Daniel was born in 1972, the year of the Rat. His Personal Gua number is 1. Based on the table on page 140, the #6 Sitting Star combines with his Personal Gua number to form the Early Heaven Sitting Star combination. The floor plan of Daniel's home with the natal flying stars chart superimposed on it is shown above right. As you can see, the #6 Sitting Star is located in the study. Thus, to improve his chances of finding Ms Right, Daniel should try to spend more time in his study, or work in his study.

The #6 Sitting Star falls in Daniel's study—if he spends more time there, he could attract a partner.

The stars and you

Your Personal Gua number essentially is a means of identifying you within a natal flying stars chart. In advanced flying stars, the Personal Gua number is used to reference the various individuals within a home, and to fine-tune things like which room the person should sleep in. It is also sometimes used for divination purposes, whereby the star combinations in the house and their interactions with the Personal Gua of each member of the family can be used to ascertain information about their lives or endeavors.

It is easy for beginners to get carried away with Personal Gua numbers and to infer all kinds of information from the natal chart of the house, often incorrectly.

Use your Personal Gua only in the manner stipulated specifically in the technique. As you advance in your knowledge of flying stars, your understanding will deepen. But at this point your Personal Gua should not be anything more than just a number to you.

Gua Gender Bender

In certain years, the Personal Gua number for each of the males and females born in that year is the same. For example, males and females who were born in 1979 have the Personal Gua number 3. However, this is not always the case. A female born in 1990, for example, has 8 as her Personal Gua number, while a male born in the same year has 1 as his.

If the wrong Gua number for your gender is used, this leads to—you guessed it—zero outcomes. Always make sure that you look at the year of birth and the gender column together when checking for your Personal Gua number.

Get creative with the qi

What do you do if the area where the Sitting Star you need to use for the Early Heaven Sitting Combination is not suitable for use as a room *per se*, or is unsuitable for study or relaxation? An example would be if the Sitting Star fell on the balcony area of your apartment or were located in the dining room or the living room. Clearly, you can't sleep there without substantial discomfort and perhaps it cannot be used for study or relaxation.

The bottom line when it comes to classical feng shui is that we always want to try to be in the right place with the right star. So the trick when it comes to spaces that cannot be "used" as rooms is simply to try to spend more time in that area.

People like to get creative with feng shui but, unfortunately, they focus on being creative in silly ways, like trying to figure out which object best represents their aims, or aiming for psychological creativity. Being creative is great, as long as you focus that creativity on thinking of ways to increase the usage of the spaces and rooms in your home that hold the qi you want.

For example, if you engage in online dating, instead of surfing the Internet in your bedroom, do it in the space or room where the Sitting Star that combines with your Personal Gua is located. If you meet someone you like, and you invite them to your home, have coffee or get to know each other in that room or that space.

If you have a laptop computer, go online dating in the rooms where the Sitting Star combines with your Personal Gua.

Need to bring Sexy back into the bedroom?

Maybe there's nothing actually wrong with your marriage, but you don't feel that it's as passionate as it was before. Or perhaps, after a spell of marriage, "that loving feeling" is not quite there, or you just want to bring that little spark back into your relationship. If your marriage is suffering in this respect, before resorting to Viagra you might want to give the annual #9 Star a chance to work a little bedroom magic.

Strictly speaking, the annual #9 Star does not directly relate to sex. But times have changed and classical feng shui practitioners have needed to be pragmatic. In the old days, a man would have one wife and several concubines. Even in the West, it was not uncommon for members of the gentry to have mistresses. If you didn't like your wife (or husband) then, you could find an alternative. Today this is less acceptable, so classical feng shui practitioners have had to be a bit ingenious (but not overly creative, naturally) in the use of flying stars.

"The annual #9 Star represents the sheng qi (growth qi) of the year but also governs happy events"

The annual #9 Star represents the sheng qi (growth qi) of the year but also governs happy events. In the old days, a happy event was almost always the birth of a child, and that of course depended on good marital relations, so in the modern application of classical feng shui the annual #9 Star is seen as a star that can help perk up or bring some passion back to the relationship.

To make use of the annual #9 Star to bring sexiness back to your relationship, you obviously need to sleep in that room with your other half, or the qi isn't getting a chance to work. But what if the annual #9 Star is in the broom closet or the storeroom? While a broom closet may be appealing for novelty's sake, using it on a regular basis just so you can tap into the benefits of the annual #9 Star does not make a lot of sense.

One way to get around this problem if you don't have an available bedroom where the annual #9 Star resides is to use the small Tai Ji technique (see page 162). This involves subdividing your bedroom into nine mini-palaces and looking for the annual #9 Star location.

If you just don't talk anymore

Love and romance aren't just for the singletons. Those in a committed relationship also want to have love and romance in their life, even though they have already found their other half. Conflicts, disagreements, misunderstandings, or lack of communication can often jettison a marriage or relationship before you can say Five Yellow. So if you find you and your other half just don't quite seem to be getting along anymore, before you decide you may have picked the wrong person, check to see if the problem is your shared home's feng shui.

This is especially the case if your relationship only started to deteriorate recently, for example coinciding with the change to a new year, switching rooms, or a move to a different home. These are usually good indications that the problem may be in the feng shui of the home, and chances are the problem is due to the annual #3 Star, also known as the 3 Jade Star. This is the star of arguments, disputes, disharmony, and poor communication. When this star is located in your bedroom (where you both sleep, thus affecting the two of you), then that is the reason you have arguments and disputes with your other half.

The influence of the annual #3 Star is usually more significant and pronounced if the star has been activated. Movement typically will activate or trigger the star, so any renovations, changing the furniture around in the room, or even nailing something to the wall can trigger the unfavorable qi.

Diagnosing and solving an annual #3 Star problem

To determine whether the cause of the strain in your relationship is the annual #3 Star, you first need to determine its location. Refer to the

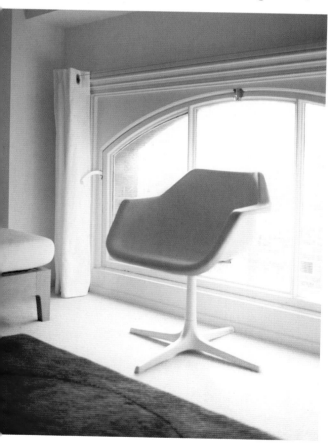

A red carpet or rug links with the Fire element, which can burn out the negative influence of the annual #3 Star in your home.

annual flying stars reference table (see page 98) to determine the location of the annual #3 Star, and then check to see if it is located in the bedroom you share with your partner (see page 99) for how to superimpose the annual flying stars chart on the floor plan). If it is located there, then this unfavorable star is likely to be the source of your quarrels.

The good news is that the star only occupies that room for the year, so you and your partner need to exhibit some tolerance or try to keep the peace only until the star shifts position again at the start of each new year. Alternatively, you could both move to another room for the year.

Elemental cure: However, if you do not think that you can keep things together, then implement an elemental cure instead. The 3 Jade Star represents the element of Wood, so Fire will weaken this Wood star. An oil lamp that is kept burning is the best cure, but this can pose safety issues, especially in a bedroom. So your next best option (although it is not a significant cure) is to lay a red carpet or place a large red rug in the room, or put a red rug at the entrance to the bedroom. However, as the problem is only temporary (because it is only an annual star), moving rooms or just learning to be more patient and tolerant may be an easier and arguably more efficacious method.

Sometimes the solution to a problem in feng shui is to get the individuals to be proactive with their own behavior. In dealing with problems that relate to relationships in particular, how we handle ourselves is as important as the circumstances in which we find ourselves.

Example: Tom and Lisa, a married couple, have recently been having a lot of squabbles. The floor plan of their house is shown on page 146, with the annual flying stars chart for 2008 superimposed. The bedroom

Myth or truth?

Water on the right of the home or main door leads to a roving eye

This is an infamous old wives' tale that has somehow developed a life of its own. There is absolutely nothing in the texts of classical feng shui that states definitively that water on the right side of the house or main door results in an unfaithful husband. A roving eye or unfaithful husband is more likely to be caused by an overactive annual #4 Star or a badly supported #4 Sitting Star. The annual #4 Star can reside in the left, right, front, or back of a home, and will be activated if there is active water in that area. So don't be in a hurry to dig up the pond on the right side of your house or main door without first checking if it coincides with the location of the annual #4 Star or the #4 Sitting Star in your home. There is no one-size-fits-all formula in classical feng shui that will guarantee that a partner won't stray.

The annual #3 Star can cause separation in a relationship.

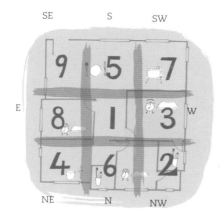

SE   S   SW

E   W

NE   N   NW

The annual #3 Star falls in Tom and Lisa's bedroom. They need to put a red rug or carpet in the room to negate its bad effects.

is located in the west palace of the house, which is also where the annual #3 Star is located in 2008. To solve the problem, they can move to an alternative bedroom or, if that isn't possible, put a red rug or carpet in the room to help temper the effects of the annual #3 Star. A table lamp with a red shade would also help reduce some of the star's effects.

The tiresome threesome

Three people do not a marriage make. The presence of a third party is a serious problem that can place significant pressure on a relationship and in some cases jeopardize it entirely. The "usual suspects" who imperil relationships by being the "third party" include the old flame who reappears on the scene, and the disgruntled and vengeful former spouse hell-bent on ruining the marriage. It doesn't always have to be someone from the past, of course—it could be work colleagues or people met in the course of a new job who place a strain on the relationship.

Myth or truth?

Mirrors in the bedroom lead to third parties

You may have heard that mirrors in the bedroom cause problems with a third party, because the reflection of the bed in the mirror makes the room too crowded. But if a mirror in the dining room means "abundant food," then surely a mirror in the bedroom should also mean "abundant passion and sex"? Why are mirrors good in one situation but not in another? This is another feng shui love myth that has been perpetuated through a combination of Chinese superstition and the overactive imagination of some New Age feng shui practitioners. These days, the myth has been extended to not having a television in your bedroom or in front of your bed.

The logical reason for avoiding mirrors in the bedroom is that they make the room very yang, because mirrors reflect light. So if you sleep in a room with a lot of mirrors, you may experience disrupted or poor-quality sleep owing to the glare from the sunlight hitting the mirrors at sunrise. It doesn't mean you can't have any mirrors in the room—it just means that having, say, an entire wall of mirrors or a mirror ceiling may not be so good for sleep if it causes morning sunlight to be reflected onto the bed. Some people like having mirrors in the bedroom and actually feel that it facilitates their relationship. As long as it doesn't disrupt your sleep, it's no big deal.

Most of the time a problem with a third party in the relationship is due to negative Peach Blossom Stars—in other words, too much attraction. The other possibility is an overactive annual #4 Star. Like the annual #3 Star, it is linked with the element Wood. When a lot of Water is placed at the location of the annual #4 Star, this creates a situation of floating Wood. A water lily is an example of this. When Wood floats it has no roots, no attachment, and is not "loyal." Thus, when the annual #4 Star is affected by Water, then straying, infidelity, third parties, and roving eyes are the outcome.

An overactive annual #4 Star can create conditions for infidelity—or three people in a relationship.

You will have to check for both these problems before you can nip the Peach Blossom problem in the bud. You'll need the floor plan of your house that has the annual flying stars chart superimposed (see page 99) and the floor plan of your house with the 24 Mountains demarcated (see pages 62–3).

Diagnosing and fixing an annual #4 Star problem

First, look for a problem with the annual #4 Star. Refer to the floor plan of your house with the annual flying stars chart for the appropriate year superimposed, and find the annual #4 Star. Is it located in a place with a water feature? For example, is it in the living room where there is an aquarium? Or is it perhaps in a bathroom where there is a bathtub? Is there a pond outside the palace where the annual #4 Star is located? What about natural water, such as a stream or lake? If any of these features is located at or outside the palace where the annual #4 Star is residing, the star has become overactive and is the cause of the third-party problems.

If the presence of water is owing to an aquarium in that room, then the solution is easy enough: Drain the aquarium or move it to another room where the qi is more conducive to Water. If the water is external in nature, then close the curtains in this room and keep the windows closed. As far as possible, you want to keep this room still and quiet, with minimal use.

Of course, in addition to resolving the problem caused by the feng shui, you need to be proactive in resolving the underlying problem. Watching your own behavior, making sure you don't send out the wrong signals (especially around the opposite sex), and avoiding places like

If your Peach Blossom Star, or your partner's, resides in your bedroom, remove any water features there to minimize bad romance luck.

nightclubs and bars (where it's easy to accidentally find yourself in a compromising situation) are some of the steps you can take to prevent further problems. And, of course, it goes without saying that spending more time with your other half is a good way to combat the problem of an overactive annual #4 Star. I say to clients, just because you have the seven-year itch doesn't mean you have to scratch.

Neutralizing the Peach Blossom Star

What if there's no indication that the annual #4 Star is being activated? Then the problem is probably being caused by either your Personal Peach Blossom Star or your partner's. To tackle this problem, you need first to find the location of the Personal Peach Blossom Star for each of you, and then take it out!

To do this, use the floor plan with the 24 Mountains demarcated (see pages 62–3). Determine the animal sign (Earthly Branch—see page 174) of your partner and yourself, and then find your Personal Peach Blossom Star and your partner's using the table on page 136.

Once you have determined the location of the Personal Peach Blossom Star for yourself and your partner, you can "neutralize" the stars' effects. Using your floor plan, determine which room or area of the home each of the two Personal Peach Blossom Stars falls within. If you're lucky and you and your partner are born in the same year or the same grouping, you'll share the Personal Peach Blossom Star. If not, you'll need to tackle the two stars separately.

In the room or area where each Personal Peach Blossom Star resides, make sure there is no water feature, such as an aquarium or water plants. Next, place more yin objects, such as tall cabinets, heavy furniture, or a large chest of drawers, in the room or area. You don't need to cram it full, but just make sure the objects in the room are fairly large and weighty. One tall cabinet will usually do. This will neutralize the effects of the Peach Blossom Star and reduce the problem of unwanted attraction or interference from amorous third parties.

Of course, it is also important that individuals take responsibility for their actions. Your own behavior and response to the unwanted attraction or interference from the third party is as important as tackling the feng shui aspect.

Making a connection

Classical feng shui is very helpful when it comes to keeping a relationship strong, because it focuses on helping you retain that loving feeling within the relationship. In fact, it captures the essence not just of what keeps a relationship going, but also of what brings us to someone in the first place: connection and affinity. The concept of love that many people envisage in a relationship essentially relates to the idea of a soul mate—a person who understands you and with whom you connect at all levels, emotionally, psychologically, intellectually, and physically. Since classical feng shui places so much emphasis on affinity and connection (Ren Yuan), it is, arguably, very useful in the actual pursuit of true love.

Myth or truth?

Water in the bedroom is bad "love" feng shui

Logically, having a water feature or aquarium in your bedroom is a bad idea because it's noisy. Disrupted sleep leaves you temperamental and likely to argue with your other half. However, it's not the water's fault, it's the noise. Besides, if we took that argument about water being bad in the bedroom to its logical conclusion, then the glass of water on your nightstand is the reason you quarreled with your spouse this morning.

Water in the bedroom need not be banned, though you might want to avoid any water feature that is noisy. Water features in the bedroom are only a bad idea if the bedroom is in a palace where Water should not be placed, such as the northwest, west, northeast, and south.

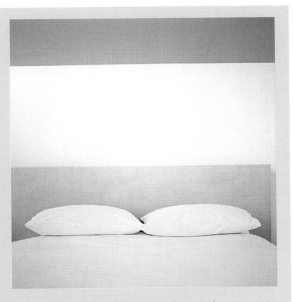

Protect the tranquility of the bedroom by banishing noisy water features.

Chapter 6
Feng Shui for Health, Vitality, and Rejuvenation

Aspiring only to have wealth, rather than good relationships or positive health, cannot be said to be the measure of a good life in feng shui. There's an old saying in feng shui that "Too much wealth deteriorates the health." By using feng shui, you can make your home a place that supports your goals in life and propels you toward your grandest dreams, but which also rejuvenates your mind, body, and spirit, bringing happiness, health, and prosperity.

The rule of five generations

There are many reasons why health in particular should never be ignored in the feng shui equation of a home. People often forget that having wealth without the capacity or ability to enjoy it is comparable to not having the money at all.

A professional feng shui consultant will always look into health matters as part of a holistic approach to the feng shui of a property. Even if the owner doesn't see this as a priority, the consultant will recommend and implement changes to take into account health considerations.

How does classical feng shui define health? In this context health relates to the concepts of longevity and prosperity. Longevity is often defined through the phrase "five generations seated in one hall," meaning that a person not only lives long enough to see their great-grandchild, but that they and their children and their children's children are fertile and are able to perpetuate the family name through offspring. And, of course, in order to have a long life, you need to have good health.

Health and wealth are intrinsically connected in classical feng shui—money grows through generations of good relationships.

Prosperity, on the other hand, relates to the ability not only to have wealth, but to enjoy one's wealth through a long life and, in addition, to have good descendant luck—meaning that you have offspring to inherit your wealth and carry on the wealth to the next generation.

Thus, according to the traditional viewpoint in classical feng shui, not living long enough to enjoy your money or to see your great-grandchildren, or having no one to inherit your money or take your wealth to the next generation, is not by any measure considered a "good life." In fact, if a person has money but a short life, or money but no one to inherit it, it is regarded as unfavorable. These are considered hallmarks of "average quality" health at best.

Of course, nowadays it is very rare for anyone to live long enough to see "five generations sitting in one hall," especially if you live in the West, where people are traditionally getting married later in life and having children much later. So being able to see your grandchild born would probably be considered "good."

Also, these days, professional feng shui consultants focus on a different concept of health. We tend to deploy feng shui for preventative purposes (keeping the person healthy and minimizing their health issues) and to help them avoid accidents, injuries, and physical harm. A house with good feng shui not only brings prosperity to the residents in terms of wealth, but also keeps them in good shape physically, mentally active and alert, and, most importantly, emotionally contented and happy.

Classical feng shui and your physician

The techniques I have shared with you here are mainly to help you tap into favorable qi, to help in maintaining good health, rejuvenating yourself, recovering from the grind of daily life, and promoting more robust health. In cases of minor ailments, classical feng shui techniques can help speed up recovery and healing, and minimize health complications.

Feng shui influences one third of the outcomes in your life. The other two thirds are your heaven luck (shown here by the dragon), and the luck you make through your own decisions.

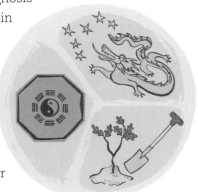

However, these methods should never be a substitute for professional medical diagnosis, advice, and treatment or be used as cures for health problems. They must always be used in tandem with a proper diagnosis by a medical professional, in the same way as you would use vitamin supplements. In the case of any health emergency, please do not try to use classical feng shui or, worse, ring your feng shui consultant—see your physician instead!

Similarly, just because you have implemented classical feng shui techniques to help promote robust health, that does not mean you should give up your gym membership or live on junk food for the rest of your life. Remember, classical feng shui only governs 33 percent of the outcomes in life. Your own actions, your man luck, play an equally important role.

You should also be aware that you will not enjoy good health instantaneously. A bad knee, back pain, or chronic ill health will not vanish overnight. The effects of classical feng shui generally require time, especially when you are using the natal flying stars chart rather than the annual stars. So you must be patient. Use classical feng shui together with your physician's advice or medication, plus a general regime of exercise and diet that are good for health.

Eat, sleep, and be healthy

In classical feng shui, certain features or rooms in a home are linked to specific areas of our life. In Chapter 3, I explained that the main door and the workroom or study room are the key home areas that relate to wealth. The emphasis in Chapter 4 was on your home's work areas, such as the study, home office, or workroom, and on the stars in these rooms, since the focus was on using feng shui to support your career goals. Chapter 5 concentrated on the bedroom, as the center for love and relationships. When it comes to health, we always look at the kitchen and the bedrooms. In other words, the focus is on where you make the food you eat and where you sleep and rejuvenate yourself.

Why focus on the kitchen and bedrooms?

You might wonder why classical feng shui chooses to focus on eating and sleeping. The rationale is really quite simple. Food is necessary for

Always check the feng shui of your bedroom by checking its flying stars—this reveals the good or poor health potential that this room offers you.

Myth or truth?

Should you double your food for extra auspiciousness?

In New Age feng shui, it is common to recommend placing a mirror in the dining room in order to create the illusion of twice as much food. Having lots of food symbolizes abundance, which is an indication of prosperity and wealth. However, having a table groaning with food (whether doubled in a mirror or not) doesn't mean that your house has more qi to go around. The food reflected in the mirror does not in itself emit qi. It is just a reflection.

Of course, from an aesthetic standpoint, having a mirror in the dining room can give the optical illusion of a larger room and this can be nice to have in a home. So go ahead and place a mirror in your dining room if you want to. Just remember, it has nothing to do with classical feng shui.

survival, but it also makes the difference between good health and poor health. In the age of the organic food revolution and advances in medical science, it has become increasingly self-evident that what we eat—what we put into our bodies—impacts significantly on our health. Classical feng shui is thus concerned with the qi that is prevalent in the place where we prepare our food: the kitchen.

In addition, human beings require sleep in order to enable the body to rejuvenate and repair itself. Rest is vital when the body is stressed or damaged by illness. Sufficient sleep has been proven to be integral not just to good health, but also to the ability to perform well at work. Classical feng shui recognizes the importance of good sleep, and so is concerned with the quality of the qi within the bedroom, which is where we sleep and rest.

Hence, whenever we want to tackle health issues using feng shui, the first port of call is always to check the feng shui of these two rooms. In this chapter, I focus mainly on the best places to locate the bedroom for optimum health and rejuvenation, and also on the types of health problems that certain flying stars or flying stars combinations can cause. As for the kitchen, the focus is not so much on flying stars as on making sure you do not breach any of the rules of internal forms. This is because the principles relating to the flying stars that can and cannot appear in the kitchen are quite complex and confusing to beginners.

To protect and improve health with classical feng shui, we focus on the kitchen and bedrooms.

Spaces for rest and rejuvenation

Bedrooms, reading rooms, spaces to chill out, and meditation or yoga rooms are just some examples of rooms and spaces that we associate with health in classical feng shui. If you don't have a reading room or a meditation or yoga room, or if you live in a small house or apartment, your personal bedroom is what matters most when it comes to your health.

Accordingly, the first step toward good health is to insure that these rooms (or any other rooms you use for relaxation or passive activity) are located in areas of the home that have energies conducive to relaxation, rest, and rejuvenation.

Creating a home that will rejuvenate you means checking your bedroom's "feng shui" health first.

Looking for Sitting Stars

For passive or yin activities, we like to have the yin energies of the Sitting Star. We are not looking at just any old Sitting Star—we want the yin energies of the most timely and benevolent Sitting Stars for the period. That means the #8, #9, and #1 Sitting Stars, as we are now in period 8 (2004–2023).

When you use the #8 Sitting Star (and, to a lesser extent, #9 and #1 Sitting Stars), you are tapping into energies that are conducive to longevity and good health. They also encourage people luck—positive relationships with other members of your family. And as the Sitting Star governs descendant luck, married couples who are trying to start a family or who want to add to their family should try to locate their marital bedroom in a room with good Sitting Stars.

First, take your house floor plan that has the natal flying stars chart of your home superimposed (see pages 56–60). Look for the #8 Sitting Star. Remember, Sitting Stars are indicated by the numbers in the top left corner of each grid box. Circle the #8 Sitting Star with a colored pen.

#8 Sitting Star in your bedroom

If the #8 Sitting Star is located in your bedroom (as in the lefthand home shown below), then you are already tapping into energies that are conducive to good health and favorable people luck. All you have to do in that case is make sure that your bed is positioned properly so that it does not breach any of the rules on bedroom forms.

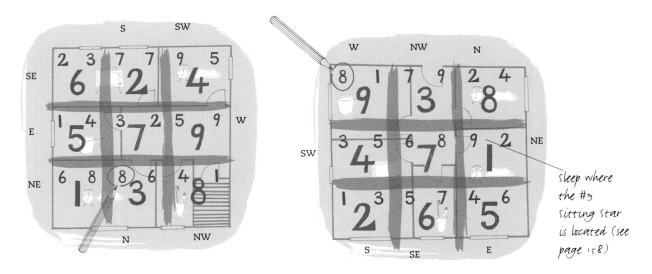

sleep where the #9 sitting star is located (see page 158)

#8 Sitting Star in your potential bedroom

If the #8 Sitting Star is not located in your bedroom, is it located in a room that is not your personal bedroom but could be used as your bedroom? If so, then all you need to do is change rooms—make the room where the #8 Sitting Star is located your bedroom and sleep there. You will immediately access the energies conducive to good health and good people luck.

#8 Sitting Star in a usable room

If the #8 Sitting Star is not located in your present bedroom, nor in a room that you can use as a bedroom, but is in a usable room (meaning it is not a storeroom or a bathroom), then you may wish to convert the room into a reading room, a meditation room, a place to chill out, listen to music, or take a nap, or a relaxation room. This way, you can still tap into the favorable energies of the #8 Sitting Star.

The home at top left is period 7, facing S1. The #8 Sitting Star is in the bedroom, so the occupants benefit from good health. In the home top right, which is period 7, facing NW 2/3, the #8 Sitting Star is in the kitchen, which can't be converted to a quiet room or bedroom. Instead, health luck can be activated by sleeping in the room with the #9 Sitting Star.

#9 or #1 Sitting Star in your bedroom or potential bedroom

If the #8 Sitting Star is not located in your present bedroom, nor in a room that you can use, you may be able to tap into the #9 and #1 Sitting Stars instead. Find the #9 Sitting Star or the #1 Sitting Star on your floor plan with the natal flying stars chart superimposed, and circle them in a different color. If either of these stars is located in your personal bedroom, or in a room that is a bedroom, or in a room that can be converted into a bedroom, then all you have to do is move into that room and use it as your personal bedroom. An example of this is the righthand illustration on page 157.

#8, #9, and #1 Sitting Stars not in usable rooms

Some homes will have the #8, #9, and #1 Sitting Stars located in rooms that cannot be used for sleeping or for relaxation activities, or in missing palaces. In that case, you have to look for a neutral Sitting Star—during period 8, it is the #6 Sitting Star.

Example: Joan and her partner live in a two-story house. It faces south 2 and is a period 7 property. The natal flying stars chart of Joan's house is shown opposite (lefthand illustration).

Joan has superimposed the natal flying stars chart of the house onto the floor plans of her house. As we are looking at the bedrooms, we will look mainly at the floor plan for the upper level of the house (see righthand illustration opposite).

The best bedroom for good health and fertility for both Joan and her partner would be in the south sector, where the #8 Sitting Star is located. As we can see from the floor plan, Joan has a bedroom there that she can use so she and her partner should preferably sleep in that bedroom.

However, the rooms in the northeast and the west are also usable as bedrooms, as these two rooms are where the #9 Sitting Star and #1 Sitting Star are located. These rooms would be used if, because of internal forms or external forms, the south palace bedroom could not be used.

Joan and her partner can also use the northeast and the west palace rooms as a meditation corner, a relaxation room, or a yoga room.

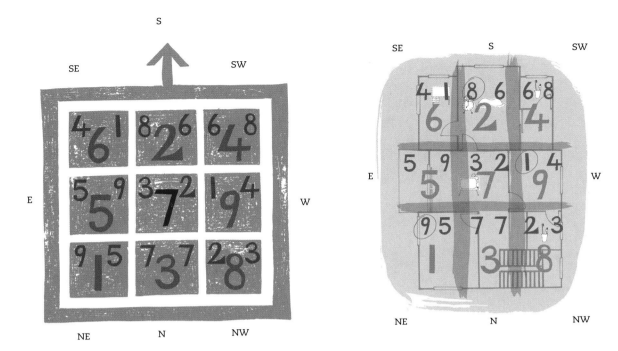

Joan's house faces S2 and is period 7. The northeast and west palaces are best used for relaxation or to locate a home gym to support good health in their household.

Alternatively, they could place their treadmill and other home gym equipment in one of these rooms, as these are activities that are related to health and rejuvenation.

I'm already in the #8 but all is not well

If you're already sleeping in the #8 Sitting Star room, but you're still always getting sick, you're squabbling constantly with family members, or you and your partner just can't seem to get in the family way, the likely cause here is external forms. They are likely to be negative, causing the #8 Sitting Star to emit negative rather than positive, benevolent qi, or they may be weakening the #8 Sitting Star.

Typical culprits might be broken, bald (without vegetation), or rocky mountains within view of the bedroom or sharp features like an angular roof, electrical pylons, or a corner from another house pointing at the palace where the bedroom is located.

If you have a pond or lake within sight or in the immediate vicinity of the bedroom where the #8 Sitting Star is located, the energies of this Sitting Star will have been diminished, as Sitting Stars are not receptive toward Water or other yang forms. A busy road with heavy traffic

Check your external forms as well as your flying stars—plants, shrubs, and trees can help minimize any negativity.

running right alongside your bedroom is also a yang form and will diminish the effectiveness of the #8 Sitting Star.

You can't fix this problem with external forms, of course, unless you have the ability to bulldoze an entire mountain, demolish your neighbor's house, or fill in a pond. And it is even harder to fix if you live in an apartment building. Therefore, your best approach would be to adopt offensive tactics (see page 93) and move into another room. You have options available to you, notably the #9 and #1 Sitting Stars, so follow the path of least resistance and simply switch rooms.

Remember, a less favorable star with no negative external forms is definitely better than a favorable star influenced by negative external forms or, worse, negated by the wrong external forms.

Dealing with health issues

The previous section assumes that you do not have any significant health-related issues, are looking for a way to maintain your health and enjoy good relationships and people luck, and therefore need only a "generic" feng shui health fix. In this section, I look at some specific issues that feng shui consultants regard as associated with health, and explain how you can tackle the problem using classical feng shui. Most problems related to health, be it mental or physical, can be traced to the kitchen or bedroom, so a lot of the fixes will be focused on these two areas.

Here are several health issues that feng shui consultants typically have to deal with in a routine consultation. Tick any that relate to you, and find the solutions on the pages indicated.

Problem	Solution
● *I have niggling bad health, frequent illnesses, or a lack of energy.*	See "Always sick?" (below).
● *I'm accident-prone—I'm always getting injured playing sports, or I fall or am prone to nicks and cuts at work or at home.*	See "Accident-prone?" (page 163).
● *I have difficulty sleeping or insomnia.*	See "Difficulty sleeping?" (page 164).
● *I often have headaches or migraines.*	See "It's all in your head" (page 166).

Always sick?

● *I have niggling bad health, frequent illnesses, or a lack of energy.*

If the above applies to you, the problem is most likely in your bedroom. Frequent illness (in other words, you are ill at least once a month) is typically caused by the #2 Sitting Star. Wherever the #2 Sitting Star is located in a home, that area is considered the illness sector. As a general rule, you should never sleep in a bedroom with a #2 Sitting Star.

When the #2 Sitting Star falls in a bedroom of this period 6, NW2/3-facing property, it can be bad news for health matters. If possible, sleep in other bedrooms, or at least move the bed (see below).

As far as possible, the best way to overcome this problem is to switch bedrooms. Try to move into a bedroom where the #8, #9, or #1 Sitting Star is located.

The small Tai Ji technique

If you have no choice but to sleep in this room, you will need to use the small Tai Ji technique to reposition your bed. Superimpose the natal flying stars chart of the property over your bedroom, dividing it into nine mini-palaces. Look for the one where the #6 or #8 Sitting Star is located, and position your bed there.

Example: After superimposing the natal chart onto his apartment floor plan, Tony discovers that his bedroom is located where the #2 Sitting Star resides, which is the east palace. Tony has no other place to locate his bedroom as he lives in a small apartment.

To use the small Tai Ji technique, Tony simply superimposes the natal flying stars chart of his apartment over his bedroom, dividing it into nine mini-palaces. He then locates his bed where the #6 or #8 Sitting Star is located, as shown below left and below right respectively.

Elemental cure: If moving the bed is not possible, then an elemental cure could be resorted to. The #2 Sitting Star is an Earth element star and thus is weakened by the element of Metal. Placing a shelf in the room and filling it with brassware, pewterware, sports trophies, sports medals, bottle-cap collections, metal picture frames, or any large metal objects should help.

If your bedroom is located where the #2 Sitting Star is and you can't move rooms, use the small Tai Ji technique and move the bed to the place of the #6 or #8 Sitting Star.

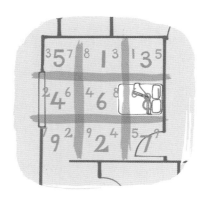

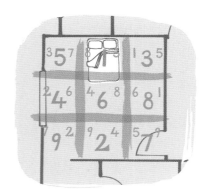

Accident-prone?

● *I'm accident-prone—I'm always getting injured playing sports, or I fall or am prone to nicks and cuts at work or at home.*

If this applies to you, then the solution will involve changes in your bedroom. The seriously accident-prone will find that they are often in hospital for broken limbs, are frequently involved in car accidents, are easily injured during routine sports or daily activities (such as twisting their ankle while shopping, or cutting themselves in the kitchen), or are prone to industrial mishaps and occupational injuries.

Displaying a trophy creates an elemental cure for the negative #2 Sitting Star.

The culprit in such an instance is the #5 Sitting Star, also known as the 5 Yellow Sitting Star. The 5 Yellow Star is the most negative star in flying stars feng shui. If you sleep in a bedroom where this star is located, you will find that you are particularly accident-prone. In itself, the #5 Sitting Star should not cause particularly serious injury, but if you happen also to have negative external forms outside the bedroom where this star is located, then the injuries from your clumsiness or carelessness will generally be more serious and severe.

Negative external forms that will trigger the #5 Sitting Star include pylons and electrical poles, a neighbor's sharp roof corner, or a sharp building corner, visible bald, rocky, or chipped mountains, abandoned buildings, or a dead tree outside the palace where the #5 Sitting Star is located. So if you are sleeping in the #5 Sitting Star bedroom and you see any of these negative external forms, you are being negatively affected by the energies of the #5 Sitting Star.

How do you solve this problem? Like the #2 Sitting Star, the #5 Sitting Star is best dealt with using offensive tactics. Move out of the bedroom into another bedroom if you can. If you can't, then use the small Tai Ji technique (see opposite) to place your bed in the mini-palace where the #8 Sitting Star is located.

Beware negative forms such as pylons, cables, and trees in combination with a #5 Sitting Star, as these magnify its bad effects.

Elemental cure: If you cannot do either of the above, then resort to an elemental cure. Place a shelf in the room, and load it with lots of metal objects like metal picture frames, brassware, pewterware, or silverware. Alternatively, you can sleep in a bed with a brass or other metal frame.

Difficulty sleeping?

● *I have difficulty sleeping.*

If the above describes you, there are several possible reasons for the problem.

Sleeping in a metal-framed bed protects the sleeper from the effects of the negative #5 Sitting Star.

Negative stars

Let's start with problems brought about by negative stars. Check your bedroom's flying stars for the following scenarios. (Note: in a combination, the Sitting Star is the first and the Facing Star the second star.)

• I am sleeping in a room with a #5 Sitting Star or #5 Facing Star.
• I am sleeping in a room with a #3 Sitting Star or #3 Facing Star.
• I am sleeping in a room with a #2 Sitting Star or a #2 Facing Star.
• I am sleeping in a room with a #2–#3 or #3–#2 combination.
• I am sleeping in a room with a #2–#5 or #5–#2 combination.
• I am sleeping in a room with a #3–#5 or #5–#3 combination.

If you answered yes to any of the above descriptions of the flying stars in your bedroom, then the source of your sleep problems clearly is the agitated energies of these negative stars.

Problematic internal forms

If you answered no to all the above, then your sleeping problems are likely to be related to the internal forms of the bedroom. Since a bedroom is a place of rest, we like it to be generally yin in nature. That means that it should not have too many windows or mirrors. If you have too many windows, the sleep problem could be caused by the room being too yang during the day, when the early morning sun hits the bedroom. And because mirrors reflect sunlight, they intensify the yang nature of the bedroom. If you have this problem, it is simple enough to solve—invest in some black-out curtains or shades.

Another internal form that could be the cause of problematic sleep is a room that is *too* yin in nature. This means that

Read my lips

Red or reddish lips (minus lipstick, obviously) indicate coughs and colds. If your lips are dark (blackish or purple), this indicates a likely problem with your stomach that may occur within the next week or so.

during the day, even with the curtains open, it is dark and gloomy, and it may possibly have a dank, damp, or musty scent. If the room is also an irregular shape (such as triangular, or with lots of awkward corners) or has a sloping or low ceiling, this also contributes to sleeping problems. Because the qi in the room is suppressed and intensely concentrated on the occupant, this makes the person agitated, emotional, and so unable to sleep well.

Taking action

As a general rule, a bedroom with any of these problems—a negative star, such as the #2, #3, or the #5 Star, a negative star combination, or negative internal forms—should not be occupied. It is always advisable to use a different room as far as possible, particularly if the resident is someone who is ailing, generally frail, or elderly.

However, if the situation cannot be helped, then positioning the bed in a favorable mini-palace using the small Tai Ji technique (see page 162) can reduce the impact of the negative room.

It is not advisable to renovate the room in order to alter the shape or change the ceiling, because if this is done without proper date selection, it will end up activating the negative stars and agitating the negative energies even more.

Sleeping in a bedroom with too many windows disturbs the yin of this room—and your night's sleep.

It's all in your head

● *I often have headaches or migraines.*

The ear test

 A quick way to make sure that all is well internally is to check your ears. The ears represent the immune system in general, but also the kidneys, which are important organs for filtering toxins and impurities in the body. If your ears are markedly darker than your complexion when you look at them in the morning, it can mean that the toxins in your body are not being excreted from your system, and that your kidneys may be giving you problems. Generally, you may become more prone to illness. If your ears are a lighter color than your complexion, then all is well.

If you are frequently a victim of headaches and migraines and your physician can find no serious medical reason for your problem, the feng shui of your home or bedroom could be the cause of your problem. The #6 Star, which is also known as the 6 White Star, relates to the head in classical feng shui. When this star, specifically the #6 Sitting Star, is negatively affected by internal forms or appears in an unfavorable combination, headaches, migraines or other head-related problems like dizziness are the outcome.

To ascertain where the problem lies, you will need to examine the #6 Sitting Star and also the internal forms in the bedroom. Take out your floor plan that has your home's natal flying stars chart superimposed (see pages 56–60). Find the location of the #6 Sitting Star, and look to see whether any of these scenarios applies to your home:

- The #6 Sitting Star is located in your bedroom.
- The #6 Sitting Star is located in one of the other bedrooms.
- The #6 Sitting Star appears in combination with the #5 Facing Star.
- The #6 Sitting Star is located in the kitchen.

#6 Sitting Star in a bedroom

If the #6 Sitting Star is located in your bedroom, or one of the other bedrooms, then you will need first to check the internal forms of the bedroom by asking yourself the following questions:

- Are there any sloping ceilings in the room?
- If so, is the bed located at the lowest point of the sloping ceiling?
- Are there lots of awkward corners or an irregular ceiling?

If you have answered yes to any of the above questions, then your problem is caused by the #6 Sitting Star exerting a negative influence

Bedroom rules

When it comes to bedrooms and internal forms, there are some basic do's and don'ts integral to insuring you have the qi in these rooms that promotes rest, sleep, and relaxation.

The focus is the room itself and also the location of the bed. When we talk about the room's forms, we are not interested in the color of the walls, the color of the curtains, or any personal items (bedside tables, bookshelves) that you may have. Instead, the primary interest in usually the shape of the room and, of course, the ceiling.

Light-filled, airy bedrooms promote good feng shui.

• A good bedroom is bright and airy and has good circulation of qi, so open the windows periodically to facilitate this.
• A good bedroom has high or medium-high ceilings.
• A good bedroom is square or rectangular in shape, with no awkward corners that stick out at odd angles.
• Avoid awkward corners that make it difficult to position the bed without a corner pointing at it.
• Avoid an airless, dark, and dank room.

• Avoid having an en suite bathroom directly in front of the bedroom door.
• Avoid having beams running across the ceiling making it impossible to position a bed without a beam running above it, horizontally or vertically.
• Avoid a slanted ceiling.
• Avoid a room that is small and cramped.

owing to negative internal forms. Suppressive qi, generated by the sloping ceiling, is pressing down upon your head, causing headaches or migraines. In an irregularly shaped room, the qi becomes erratic, and the cause of the headache is likely to be either a corner pointing at your head as you sleep or the headboard of the bed not being located against a wall.

Sometimes, headaches and migraines can be caused by a computer or television creating an excessive Fire element.

Subdivide your bedroom into nine mini-palaces using the small Tai Ji technique (see page 162), then superimpose the natal flying stars chart of the property over your bedroom. Is your computer or television in the mini-palace where the #6 Sitting Star is located? If so, then your problem is clearly caused by the #6 Sitting Star being aggravated by the Fire

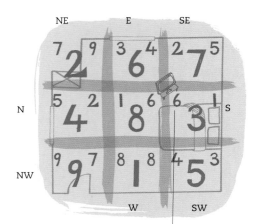

The television is positioned where the #6 Sitting Star is located, which can cause headaches and migraines.

Here, the #6 Sitting Star is located in the kitchen—another cause of migraines or headaches in this home.

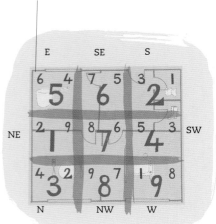

elements. Just move the television or computer and your problem should go away.

If the internal forms reveal no problem and you have no television or computer in your bedroom, look at the scenarios below to see if any is applicable.

#6 Sitting Star with #5 Facing Star

The #5 Star, be it as a Sitting Star or as a Facing Star, is regarded as a negative star. Also known as the 5 Yellow, it is a sort of troublemaker star, and when it appears in tandem with another star, it tends to affect that other star negatively. A useful analogy is to think of it as peer influence. When a good kid gets involved with a bad crowd, they end up becoming troublemakers themselves, owing to peer influence. The #5 Star has this "negative peer influence" effect on the stars with which it appears in combination.

When you have the #5 Facing Star in combination with the #6 Sitting Star, the #5 Facing Star ends up negatively influencing the #6 Sitting Star, causing the latter to exert its negative effects. Since the #6 Sitting Star relates to the head, the negative effects naturally impact on the head first, causing headaches or migraines.

If you want to be thorough, it is best to check all the bedrooms in the home for the #6–#5 combination. Also, you want to make sure that you don't see the #5–#6 combination (#5 Sitting Star with #6 Facing Star) in the bedrooms either, since this would exert a broadly similar effect. If you want to be ultra-thorough, you could also check to make sure the #6–#5 or #5–#6 combination doesn't appear in any working room (study, home office, workroom) as this would mean you would have headaches and migraines every time you tried to work.

#6 Sitting Star in the kitchen

Even if there is no #6 Sitting Star in any of the bedrooms, problems of migraines or headaches can still occur if the #6 Sitting Star is located in the kitchen. The #6 Sitting Star, being of the Wood element, is very sensitive to the influence of Fire. The stove—including the range, cooktop,

Kitchen rules

Because the kitchen is where food is prepared and stored, it is particularly important that we have the right kind of qi here. If the qi in the kitchen is negative, then the food that is prepared here is affected. Many people also tend to eat in their kitchens, so suitable and favorable qi is all the more important.

What matters is not the color of the walls, the color of the curtains, or the type of furniture you have. The placement of certain kitchen items does matter—but the type of table, chairs, utensils, and whether or not you display knives in your kitchen are not relevant to its feng shui.

I have focused on internal forms relating to the kitchen, and minimized any use of the flying stars because the rules on what kind of flying stars are permissible or favorable in a kitchen are less clear-cut than for the bedroom or main door.

Don't put the stove next to the sink

Locating a Fire element object, such as a stove, cook-top, or oven, next to a Water element object (like the sink) creates what is known as a Fire and Water clash. This may be associated with problems such as high or low blood pressure or heart-related conditions such as palpitations or cardiac arrhythmia. Make sure the sink and stove are at least 1ft (30cm) apart.

If you can't avoid the situation, put some herbs or a modest potted plant in between the two, since Wood (the plant) will moderate the clash between the Fire and Water.

Don't buy a home with a kitchen in the center

A kitchen located smack in the center of a home is a serious breach of the rules on internal forms. The center of the house is known as the central Tai Ji or Heavenly Heart and it must always be quiet, peaceful, and yin in nature. A kitchen is regarded as a very yang feature, and when it is located in the center of the home it causes the qi in the house to be disruptive, resulting in malingering health and frequent illness.

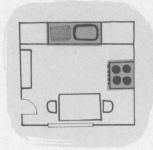

Island units should not contain stoves. The sink and stove must always be separate, as shown here (left)—never side by side.

Avoid an island with a stove

It is quite common for modern kitchens to have a central "island." If you simply have a breakfast bar on the island, that's fine. But if your stove or cooktop is located on the island, then this is a problem. The stove should always be placed against a solid wall. When you have your stove on the island, it has no rear support, is unstable, and is exposed to sha qi. This is especially the case if the back of the stove faces the kitchen entrance.

When qi affecting the stove is unstable, the food cooked on the stove is affected by negative qi, thus resulting in health problems.

Talk to Dr Nose

In the study of face reading, the nose is regarded as the health palace, so checking your nose in the mirror every morning is a good way to get a quick idea of your health.

If there is a dark patch of skin on your nose that wasn't there last week, stock up on vitamins and get ready to be ill soon. If a black spot or a mole appears on your nose, this can indicate that you may soon be in for a niggling or chronic illness that requires long-term medication.

Lines running down from the bridge of the nose are associated with back problems.

and oven—is obviously a Fire element object. When the #6 Sitting Star is in the kitchen, it is being negatively affected by the presence of the Fire element, in the form of the stove. So if the #6 Sitting Star is located in the kitchen, then this is usually the cause of headaches and migraines in the household.

Handling a problematic #6 Sitting Star

Handling a problematic #6 Sitting Star depends largely on where it is located and the nature of the problem. If it is located in a bedroom with negative internal forms, moving out of the bedroom is probably the easiest answer. Renovation is also an option, for example to straighten out the ceiling, but this can be an expensive recourse. Moving out of the room is generally an easier change to implement.

If the #6 Sitting Star is problematic through being in combination with the #5, this is slightly more difficult to tackle. Again, moving out of the room would be the best option.

In both these instances, if moving out of the room is not an option because there is no other bedroom available, the small Tai Ji technique (see page 162) can be used to improve the positioning of the bed to reduce the effects of the negativity.

Cook in the mini-palace that has the #3 or #4 Sitting Star to deal with the effects of the #6 Sitting Star.

Elemental cure: Alternatively, you could try using an elemental cure, strengthening the #6 Sitting Star, which is a Metal star, by adding more of the Metal element to the room. Use a bed with an iron or brass frame, and/or place more metal objects around the room, such as metal picture frames or a shelf with brassware, silverware, or pewterware. You can also, if space permits, place a large metal sculpture or object in the room.

If the #6 Sitting Star is located in the kitchen, this is quite a tricky problem to resolve. It does, of course, also depend on how often you cook. If you are an active and frequent cook, then the stove is likely to be affecting the #6 Sitting Star significantly. If you cook less often, then the problem is reduced in magnitude and severity. The only solution is to use the small Tai Ji technique (see page 162) to reposition the stove.

Use annual flying stars to determine the best room to sleep in to speed up the healing process.

Divide up your kitchen into nine mini-palaces, and superimpose the natal flying stars chart of the house onto the kitchen's nine mini-palaces. Now place the stove in the mini-palace that has the #3 or #4 Sitting Star in it.

Tapping into healing qi

If you are recovering from a bout of illness, if you have undergone a medical procedure, or if you will be undergoing one soon, tapping into healing qi is the key to a swift and problem-free recovery. To do this, you need to find the healing qi sector for the year, which is where the annual #6 Star is located. (You can temporarily ignore the natal flying stars chart of your house.)

The #6 Star, also known as the 6 White Star, is a Metal element star, and thus weakens the effects of the 2 Black Star, the star of illness. By tapping into the #6 Star, you are helping to rejuvenate and restore your body following injury or illness. Examples of health problems where the annual #6 Star's healing qi can be used are before or after a tonsillectomy, appendectomy, and knee surgery, and when you are recovering from a bad bout of flu or a sprained ankle.

As a general rule, any illness or injury from which recovery would take about three to six months is the type that the annual #6 Star can be used to tackle. It will help to minimize post-treatment or post-illness complications, while helping your body recover and rest. Using the annual #6 Star to help with a long-term or extremely serious illness is an unwise and incorrect use of the star.

If the annual #6 Star is located in a bedroom, then sleep in that bedroom. If it is located in a room that you can use for watching television or for convalescing by reading or taking short naps there, then use the room in that way.

Remember, no matter how effective classical feng shui can be, it is always to be used as a complement to medical advice and therapy. So if you want to recover from a knee injury, for example, don't stop doing physiotherapy because you are sleeping in the room where the annual #6 Star is located. Use classical feng shui in tandem with professional medical advice.

Example: In 2010, Janice plans to undergo knee surgery to resolve a niggling problem with her knee. She expects to be in recovery and physiotherapy for three months. In that year, the annual #6 Star falls in the southwest section of her home, where her reading room is located. Janice can either use the southwest reading room as her bedroom for the three months she'll be recovering from surgery, or rest there during the day and engage in her physiotherapy exercise in that room.

Myth or truth?

Knives and sha qi

It is a fallacy that kitchen knives should not be stored in a knife block or on a magnetic knife rack because of supposedly creating sha qi in the kitchen. The only reason for keeping the knives in drawers is for safety. Not every sharp object gives off sha qi—otherwise, we would logically not be able to have letter openers on our desks or pencils on our tables. For that matter, Chinese people would not eat with chopsticks and Westerners would be able to eat only with spoons. If we lived our lives according to the mantra that sharp equals sha, honestly, you wouldn't be able to set foot out the door of your home, or even leave your bed!

Epilogue

I hope that what you have read in this book has enabled you to explore feng shui with new insight and understanding. I hope, too, that this is only the beginning of your journey and your connection with feng shui. The question now is, where do you go from here?

It may be that whatever you have learned and been able to apply in this book is enough for you. After all, as you know by now, feng shui influences one third of our life endeavors, so if you have begun to make use of the techniques outlined in this book, you are well ahead in the game of life.

On the other hand, you may also find that your interest in classical feng shui has been piqued and you would like to know more. A good way to advance your knowledge is to broaden your reading. You may want to dip into books on Eight Mansions feng shui or more advanced books on Xuan Kong flying stars. However, as much of the information is still largely contained in Chinese language books, this can be a bit of a challenge.

I have written a beginner's text on Xuan Kong flying stars and you may find that useful. If you are looking for more ideas on how to apply feng shui to your home, you may want to look at my Feng Shui for Homebuyers series, consisting of *Feng Shui for Homebuyers: Exterior*, *Feng Shui for Homebuyers: Interior*, and *Feng Shui for Apartment Owners*. If you are interested in the face-reading aspect of Chinese metaphysics or the Chinese astrology aspect, I have two introductory books on these subjects as well, which you may find useful. A list of my books can be found at the website www.joeyyap.com. The website also contains some useful feng shui tools and calculators that you can use to explore the subject of classical feng shui further.

You could also consider taking a class on the subject, with a qualified teacher. At the same time, you can learn a lot from practice, so perhaps you might want to try out some of the techniques in this book on friends or family and observe the outcomes!

Whichever path you choose, I hope that this book has been a good companion, helping you embrace and harness the tremendous benefits of feng shui. Have fun as you continue trying out the techniques in this book and, most importantly, being open to all the possibilities that classical feng shui has to offer.

Year Pillar & Gua Number Reference Table 1920–2015

Animal	Year of Birth		Gua number for Male/Female	
Monkey	1920	Yang Metal Monkey (Geng Shen)	8	7
Rooster	1921	Yin Metal Rooster (Xin You)	7	8
Dog	1922	Yang Water Dog (Ren Xu)	6	9
Pig	1923	Yin Water Pig (Gui Hai)	2	1
Rat	1924	Yang Wood Rat (Jia Zi)	4	2
Ox	1925	Yin Wood Ox (Yi Chou)	3	3
Tiger	1926	Yang Fire Tiger (Bing Yin)	2	4
Rabbit	1927	Yin Fire Rabbit (Ding Mao)	1	8
Dragon	1928	Yang Earth Dragon (Wu Chen)	9	6
Snake	1929	Yin Earth Snake (Ji Si)	8	7
Horse	1930	Yang Metal Horse (Geng Wu)	7	8
Goat	1931	Yin Metal Goat (Xin Wei)	6	9
Monkey	1932	Yang Water Monkey (Ren Shen)	2	1
Rooster	1933	Yin Water Rooster (Gui You)	4	2
Dog	1934	Yang Wood Dog (Jia Xu)	3	3
Pig	1935	Yin Wood Pig (Yi Hai)	2	4
Rat	1936	Yang Fire Rat (Bing Zi)	1	8
Ox	1937	Yin Fire Ox (Ding Chou)	9	6
Tiger	1938	Yang Earth Tiger (Wu Yin)	8	7
Rabbit	1939	Yin Earth Rabbit (Ji Mao)	7	8
Dragon	1940	Yang Metal Dragon (Geng Chen)	6	9
Snake	1941	Yin Metal Snake (Xin Si)	2	1
Horse	1942	Yang Water Horse (Ren Wu)	4	2
Goat	1943	Yin Water Goat (Gui Wei)	3	3
Monkey	1944	Yang Wood Monkey (Jia Shen)	2	4
Rooster	1945	Yin Wood Rooster (Yi You)	1	8
Dog	1946	Yang Fire Dog (Bing Xu)	9	6
Pig	1947	Yin Fire Pig (Ding Hai)	8	7
Rat	1948	Yang Earth Rat (Wu Zi)	7	8
Ox	1949	Yin Earth Ox (Ji Chou)	6	9
Tiger	1950	Yang Metal Tiger (Geng Yin)	2	1
Rabbit	1951	Yin Metal Rabbit (Xin Mao)	4	2
Dragon	1952	Yang Water Dragon (Ren Chen)	3	3
Snake	1953	Yin Water Snake (Gui Si)	2	4
Horse	1954	Yang Wood Horse (Jia Wu)	1	8
Goat	1955	Yin Wood Goat (Yi Wei)	9	6
Monkey	1956	Yang Fire Monkey (Bing Shen)	8	7
Rooster	1957	Yin Fire Rooster (Ding You)	7	8
Dog	1958	Yang Earth Dog (Wu Xu)	6	9
Pig	1959	Yin Earth Pig (Ji Hai)	2	1
Rat	1960	Yang Metal Rat (Geng Zi)	4	2
Ox	1961	Yin Metal Ox (Xin Chou)	3	3
Tiger	1962	Yang Water Tiger (Ren Yin)	2	4
Rabbit	1963	Yin Water Rabbit (Gui Mao)	1	8
Dragon	1964	Yang Wood Dragon (Jia Chen)	9	6
Snake	1965	Yin Wood Snake (Yi Si)	8	7
Horse	1966	Yang Fire Horse (Bing Wu)	7	8
Goat	1967	Yin Fire Goat (Ding Wei)	6	9

Animal	Year of Birth		Gua number for Male/Female	
Monkey	1968	Yang Earth Monkey (Wu Shen)	2	1
Rooster	1969	Yin Earth Rooster (Ji You)	4	2
Dog	1970	Yang Metal Dog (Geng Xu)	3	3
Pig	1971	Yin Metal Pig (Xin Hai)	2	4
Rat	1972	Yang Water Rat (Ren Zi)	1	8
Ox	1973	Yin Water Ox (Gui Chou)	9	6
Tiger	1974	Yang Wood Tiger (Jia Yin)	8	7
Rabbit	1975	Yin Wood Rabbit (Yi Mao)	7	8
Dragon	1976	Yang Fire Dragon (Bing Chen)	6	9
Snake	1977	Yin Fire Snake (Ding Si)	2	1
Horse	1978	Yang Earth Horse (Wu Wu)	4	2
Goat	1979	Yin Earth Goat (Ji Wei)	3	3
Monkey	1980	Yang Metal Monkey (Geng Shen)	2	4
Rooster	1981	Yin Metal Rooster (Xin You)	1	8
Dog	1982	Yang Water Dog (Ren Xu)	9	6
Pig	1983	Yin Water Pig (Gui Hai)	8	7
Rat	1984	Yang Wood Rat (Jia Zi)	7	8
Ox	1985	Yin Wood Ox (Yi Chou)	6	9
Tiger	1986	Yang Fire Tiger (Bing Yin)	2	1
Rabbit	1987	Yin Fire Rabbit (Ding Mao)	4	2
Dragon	1988	Yang Earth Dragon (Wu Chen)	3	3
Snake	1989	Yin Earth Snake (Ji Si)	2	4
Horse	1990	Yang Metal Horse (Geng Wu)	1	8
Goat	1991	Yin Metal Goat (Xin Wei)	9	6
Monkey	1992	Yang Water Monkey (Ren Shen)	8	7
Rooster	1993	Yin Water Rooster (Gui You)	7	8
Dog	1994	Yang Wood Dog (Jia Xu)	6	9
Pig	1995	Yin Wood Pig (Yi Hai)	2	1
Rat	1996	Yang Fire Rat (Bing Zi)	4	2
Ox	1997	Yin Fire Ox (Ding Chou)	3	3
Tiger	1998	Yang Earth Tiger (Wu Yin)	2	4
Rabbit	1999	Yin Earth Rabbit (Ji Mao)	1	8
Dragon	2000	Yang Metal Dragon (Geng Chen)	9	6
Snake	2001	Yin Metal Snake (Xin Si)	8	7
Horse	2002	Yang Water Horse (Ren Wu)	7	8
Goat	2003	Yin Water Goat (Gui Wei)	6	9
Monkey	2004	Yang Wood Monkey (Jia Shen)	2	1
Rooster	2005	Yin Wood Rooster (Yi You)	4	2
Dog	2006	Yang Fire Dog (Bing Xu)	3	3
Pig	2007	Yin Fire Pig (Ding Hai)	2	4
Rat	2008	Yang Earth Rat (Wu Zi)	1	8
Ox	2009	Yin Earth Ox (Ji Chou)	9	6
Tiger	2010	Yang Metal Tiger (Geng Yin)	8	7
Rabbit	2011	Yin Metal Rabbit (Xin Mao)	7	8
Dragon	2012	Yang Water Dragon (Ren Chen)	6	9
Snake	2013	Yin Water Snake (Gui Si)	2	1
Horse	2014	Yang Wood Horse (Jia Wu)	4	2
Goat	2015	Yin Wood Goat (Yi Wei)	3	3

Please note that the date for the Chinese Solar Year starts on Feb 4. This means that if you were born in Feb 2 of 1982, you belong to the previous year, 1981.

Index

Personal favorable/unfavorable directions (East Group)

GUA	FAVORABLE				UNFAVORABLE			
	Sheng qi	Tian yi	Yan nian	Fu wei	Huo hai	Wu gui	Liu sha	Jue ming
Kan 1 Water	SE	E	S	N	W	NE	NW	SW
Zhen 3 Wood	S	N	SE	E	SW	NW	NE	W
Xun 4 Wood	N	S	E	SE	NW	SW	W	NE
Li 9 Fire	E	SE	N	S	NE	W	SW	NW

Personal favorable/unfavorable directions (West Group)

GUA	FAVORABLE				UNFAVORABLE			
	Sheng qi	Tian yi	Yan nian	Fu wei	Huo hai	Wu gui	Liu sha	Jue ming
Kun 2 Earth	NE	W	NW	SW	E	SE	S	N
Qian 6 Metal	W	NE	SW	NW	SE	E	N	S
Dui 7 Metal	NW	SW	NE	W	N	S	SE	E
Gen 8 Earth	SW	NW	W	NE	S	N	E	SE